I Was the
Samaritan Woman
at the Well

Sheila L. White

ISBN 979-8-89043-551-4 (paperback)
ISBN 979-8-89043-552-1 (digital)

Christian Faith Publishing
832 Park Avenue
Meadville, PA 16335
www.christianfaithpublishing.com

Unless otherwise indicated, all Scripture quotations are taken from the King James Version of the Bible.

Printed in the United States of America

Contents

Preface

I author this book because I have long wanted to write and share my story to help someone else. Even though this is my first published book, I believe it is God who has gifted me to write it. I believe that with the help of God's Holy Spirit, he will anoint my hands and guide my thoughts as I write my first published book. I get this book published in Jesus' name.

God began to confirm that he wanted me to write on February 1997 by providing a scholarship for me through a woman, who at the time I did not know. I found out later that she was the wife of a man who had ministered at what I call my first real church in San Francisco, California. I was a member there. My counselor and my sister had told me that they thought I would be a good writer. My sister remembered the book I wrote for my unborn son. I was sixteen. His name was Mark Anthony Porter Jr. The only child, it turned out, that I would ever birth. The book was written for my son to read when he became old enough to read. Now that he is deceased, he will never get a chance to find the pleasure that I have found in reading and writing.

The first book I wrote and illustrated has long been lost or taken over the years. I pray someday God will allow me to author the book again in dedication to my deceased son, Mark Anthony Porter Jr. I thought that as I wrote these pages, I believe there would be healing in it for me, but it was God all by himself that healed me of the grief that was restricting me, I now know, in every area of my life. My former pastor, through a counseling session about my finances, saw that I was still grieved about my son's death from April 1994. He gave me an assignment. The first instruction was to spend time in praising and worshiping my Heavenly Father. The second instruction was to go home and to have an ugly cry about the loss of my son.

Now, I decide to have a cry about every loss. I do not remember if my former pastor told me to have the ugly cry about every loss, or it was just me. I wanted any other loss that may have been hindering me gone from my life because I was ready to move forward with life. I do not know if I have the instruction in the correct order, but God knew what my pastor had instructed me to do. So I spent some time in praise and worship; and I had a good, long, ugly cry. I fell asleep in the process. I woke back up, and I continued until I felt like I had the breakthrough that I needed. Afterward, I turned my television on to Christian TV.

If I remember correctly, it was Charles Stanley's teaching on 1 Thessalonians 4:13–18:

> But I would not have you to be ignorant, brethren, concerning them which are asleep, that ye sorrow not, even as others which have no hope. For if we believe that Jesus died and rose again, even so them also which sleep in Jesus will God bring with him. For this we say unto you by the word of the Lord, that we which are alive and remain unto the coming of the Lord shall not prevent them which are asleep. For the Lord himself shall descend from heaven with a shout, with the voice of the archangel, and with the trump of God: and the dead in Christ shall rise first: Then we which are alive and remain shall be caught up together with them in the clouds, to meet the Lord in the air: and so shall we ever be with the Lord. Wherefore comfort one another with these words.

I knew this was my confirmation; I received my breakthrough. Now, when I need to share to help someone else, I can do it without tears.

I have been waiting for the right time to write. There is no right time. I just need to be obedient. This book is twenty-five years overdue. There may never be a right to start your book just start. I received my heavenly language on August 9, 1998. I thought, *Now is the time to write.* It was August 1998 that God gave me the title of this book and several of the chapter titles. Here I was in the year 2021, living in Minnesota and working on my manuscript. One of my first ladies spoke a message about no more excuses.

1

My Story

And deliver them who through fear of death
were all their lifetime subject to bondage.

—Hebrew 2:15

I write you this story because I honestly believe someone needs to hear it. If it helps but one person, then God has accomplished his purpose through me because that one person may go on to help hundreds and even thousands. God uses different people from all walks of life, and even if you tell your story or testimony to one person, I personally thank you.

I was born on a Monday in 1958 at 9:00 a.m. in Clayton, Missouri, to my mom, Rosalie White, and dad, James Smith. My parents were never married to each other. I was my mother's second child and second daughter. I am my dad's first child as far as I know. My mother went on to have seven more children.

I did not grow up in the church, but Big Mamma, my dad's mother, was a Christian. So I always had the opportunity to go to church with my Big Mamma and younger sister. You see, my Big Mamma was attempting to make up where my dad, her son, was lacking. My Big Mamma went home to be with the Lord on March 1986. I often wish my Big Mamma were still alive today to see what a difference God has made in my life. She would be blessed.

My Big Mamma was special to me because my sister and I were the only ones I could remember who called her Big Mamma. Her other grandchildren called her Mi Mi. It was as though my sister and I had our own special place with my Big Mamma because it appeared to me that as a child, my mom's mother did not really take an interest in us but a few of her other grandchildren, but we did spend time at her home. My Big Mamma was about five feet, five inches in height. She was heavily built and was always on a diet, attempting to lose weight, but I loved her the way she was. She had a beautiful smile and chocolate complexion. Big Mamma was friendly but stern. What makes me smile when I think about my Big Mamma is her relationship with God and the fact that she cared about my sister and me. I miss the fact that I never will be able to share with her how much I have learned about God and how much he loves me.

When Big Mamma died, I was just beginning to learn about the Godhead (God the Father, God the Son, and God the Holy Spirit). I am not sure if she filled a gap in my life for me, but Big Mamma and Granddaddy lived on a farm, and being on the farm was an adventurous and pleasant experience for me. I dreamed about her quite often the first few years after her death. I now understand a little more about dreams and how things happen in the spirit realm—good or bad—through your dreams. My granddaddy just died in the year 2020 at the age of ninety-nine.

I grew up in an era where Black children were taught only to speak when spoken to, and we were not allowed to express our feelings. It was not fair to always be told to shut up all the time. I thought the phrase "shut up" was cruel. I hate the phrase to this very day. Quite often, I was accused of things I did not do and sometimes receiving a whipping for another sibling's wrongdoing. Since you were told to shut up before you could say someone else did it, you received a whipping, and the truth never came out. There were times when I was accused of trying to wake my mom up while she was sleeping. If I were given the opportunity, I would have said, "Mom, I just want to help get the kitchen ready for breakfast."

The time a group of us children got a whipping for trying to wash clothes in the bathtub by stomping on the clothes in a tub of water with our feet. I would have said, "Mom, we just wanted to help you wash clothes since you are so busy taking care all of us." I would have told her, "Mom, I do not like wearing dirty clothes." Then there were the times when my older sister and the younger siblings would gang up on me whenever Mom and my stepfather would leave home. Mom would tell me that I would always go to my room when it was time for her to go away. I would have said, "Mom, this was not true. I was avoiding getting picked on and beat up by my sisters and brothers." The younger siblings did not know any better; they were just following the leader. I would be surprised if they even remember these scenarios. That is okay if they do not remember; this is my story, and I am the only one that can tell it from my view. I am not in any way trying to make anyone look bad. I am just telling my story the way that I experienced it. There was so much I would have said to my mom then and now.

I remember looking out the window of my home in Vallejo, California, having a conversation with God and asking him, when I felt rejected in relationships with a man, why did I seek attention from a different man? The answer I received while standing at that window went something like this: Maybe your mother did not want you when she was pregnant with you. I told God I heard of such things, but I never applied it to myself. I answered back: Even if that were true, my mom would not admit to it. I told God that I was going to call her the next day to see what she would say. Well, she did admit she was going to give me up for an adoption if I was a girl.

So I was a girl in my mother's womb feeling her rejection. Once I learned through the Holy Spirit what was going on with me, I had something I could pray about to get healed and delivered so I will not continue in this immoral behavior. Even though I say I did not grow up with my dad, I did spend my ninth-grade school year with him and his family. It did not have a lot of impact on me. Dad just yelled and screamed when his children did something that we were not supposed to do. We would sometimes even get a whipping by him. There was no communication there either. He was either at work or out gambling or out womanizing. So after Dad had shipped me back off to Mom's, I did not know my dad, so I attempted to have a relationship with him by pretending I had this great relationship of communication with him via the telephone or times when I would visit. I would say whatever was on my mind, but I realized very quickly that I really did not have this great relationship with Dad.

When I tried to find out something about his childhood, the walls came up, and Dad became incredibly angry and defensive. He would begin telling me what his parents did not do for him, as though that gave him an excuse not to be a good parent. The conversation was then over. I would at least like to thank my dad for allowing me to be opinionated, even though he did not care for it.

As a result of not being able to truly express my feelings and opinions with my parents or any adult, I have always had an active imagination. I was always in deep thought as a child and even now as an adult. I have had trouble with authority, but it has been through my relationship with God that allowed me to put those in authority in the right perspective. My friends and acquaintances always told me I had to have the last word. I am very outspoken.

I worked for fourteen years as a San Francisco police officer, and I was always bucking up against my supervisors or coworkers. Maybe I was always questioning what they would ask me to do. I did not disrespect them. I just had to express my opinion. It was after eight years in the police department that God began to deal with me. In my eighth year as a police officer, it was when I came to God with a broken spirit. I let go and let God. I said to God, "I am a Christian, and no one even knows it. I am angry and bitter at these people on my job, and I do not even want to let go of the anger and bitterness."

What I was talking about was what these people, my coworkers, had done to me. I was discriminated against and mistreated on the job. I was given assignments that no other female officers were given. I was called the Black militant female. It was because I was a strong-willed Black woman. It seemed almost immediately that God began to do a miraculous work in me. It was not that anything had changed in those people on my job. God changed something in me. As a result, being unable to express my feelings and opinions, I was very boisterous and opinionated, and in a paramilitary job, this did not go over very well. Thank God I was not in the armed forces.

I would have been court-martialed. God is still working with my mouth and me. I am slowly learning. I do not have to always express my opinion. I am learning to pray about things and allowing God to fight my battles.

Even though I express quite a bit of my feelings or opinions, I still held quite a bit in when it came to conversations with my mom. I do not like conflict the way I used to because my son was murdered for a minor conflict—over a box of Cheerios. A friend of mine, who helped me on the edit of my first manuscript, had me digging deeper. I am glad she told me to dig deep. This gave me a chance to express my true feelings. Mom and Dad have now transitioned to heaven, but it is sometimes good to write some things down. It is therapy of some sort. Someone in the family may read my book and have issue with it.

You see, when you are codependent, one of your traits is wanting someone to take your side of the argument. So by the person bringing this information to other people in the family, in the person's mind, it would make them look good and favorable to the receiver of the information. I would have loved to have an open and honest relationship with my mom when she was here on earth. I loved her so much. I just wanted to be close to her and be able to share things with her.

In the meanwhile, I talked to my God, who will never leave me or forsake me, nor will he betray my trust. Jesus is my Savior and my advocate. The Holy Spirit is my comforter, teacher, and guide.

You always hear the phrase "Always daddy's girl." When my dad left his first wife, I remember thinking, *Oh, wow, now I can have my dad all to myself.* Well, that, too, would never happen. My dad has passed to heaven. My God, the Father, will be all to me. Parents do the best that they know how to do. I believe my parents are fine now; they have left their fleshly bodies behind to be absent from the body to be present with our Savior. I absolutely loved them both unconditionally.

I have also learned sometimes that you may have to separate and pray for some family and friends. I also realize that we cannot live in this world alone, and I do not want to be alone. We have to be willing to forgive people just as God our Father forgives us. Matthew 6:14–15 says, "For if ye forgive men their trespasses, your heavenly Father will also forgive you: But if ye forgive not men their trespasses, neither will your Father forgive your trespasses." You do not want to risk missing heaven for some unforgiveness you chose not to forgive.

I thank God for my mom. I held her dear to my heart, and I kept her up in prayer when she was here on earth. I loved my mom with all my heart, and my mother did the best she knew how in raising her children. Since we were not allowed to express feelings when I was a child, I did grow up not being able to communicate with her. I learned about the birds and the bees from an older sister, the streets, and friends or acquaintances. The first day of my menstrual cycle, I felt shame, and I thought I had done something wrong. I told my oldest sister; she, in turn, told my mom back in those days.

So I grew up not feeling comfortable talking about my cycle and resenting the men in my life who teased me about being on the rag whenever I was not behaving in a way acceptable to them. So I did not have a mother (for whatever the reason) to talk to about things that occurred to me as a young girl as I went into puberty. Nor did I have a father whom I felt comfortable talking to about young boys. At the time, I did not understand who God was nor did I have a personal relationship with Jesus Christ, the anointed one. So you see, I was kind of left to live life alone without understanding that my Heavenly Father was there all the time.

As a consequence of my childhood, I vowed at age twelve to never to get married or to have children. I have since learned the power of words. Now, I have no children, and I have no grandchildren as far as I know. Words are powerful. We have to choose life with the words that we speak out of our mouth. Proverbs says in chapter 18, verse 21, "Death and life are in the power of the tongue: and they that love it shall eat the fruit there of."

Deuteronomy 30:19 says, "I call heaven and earth to record this day against you, *that* I have set before you life and death blessing and cursing therefore choose life, that both thou and thy seed may live."

Growing up with my older sister, it seemed she had it in for me, and whenever my mom and stepfather went out to take care of business, my oldest sister would put my only whole sister (same mom and same dad) and myself up to fight. Everyone else would gang up on me. Mom always seemed to be starting a verbal or physical fight with my stepfather when I was growing up as a child. There was a lot of chaos going on in my home because of children, a wife, and husband. So you see, this is why I vowed never to get married or have children. This vow has since been renounced. I did not see anything good about having children or being married. I do not feel this way any longer. I went on to have four husbands and a child by my first husband. So I made a vow that I never did keep even to myself, not knowing that I was an unwanted girl child in my mother's womb, which I did not realize until 1989 through the Holy Spirit revealing to me that I had a problem with rejection. The Holy Spirit will show you some things if you let him. I would attempt to fill a void that only a relationship with Jesus Christ could fill with numerous sexual relationships and four marriages. And as I write this book, I still struggled in this area until I broke free of a nine-year-plus relationship that was not working for either party involved.

If I had just listened to the shepherd that God placed me up under, I would have avoided a lot of hurt and pain for myself. My pastor told me to break up with the person. He teaches that there should be no other date but the wedding date and then comes the courtship. There is healing as I write each page. As I finally finish my manuscript, I am watchful how and who I spend my time. We must really be watchful to protect my boundaries, and we should not place ourselves into situations that are tempting and cause us to sin.

It was through an unhappy childhood that I grew independent of my family, and I lived a couple of thousand miles away for seventeen and a half years of my life. It was through being away from my family, getting saved, and attending church that I learned that I was brought up in a dysfunctional family, and God showed me that I was just as dysfunctional as the rest of my family. It was through what I call my first real church that my Heavenly Father began to make me healthier and less dysfunctional in how I deal with life.

I hold dear to my heart *Genesis 12:1–3*, where God told Abram to leave his kinfolks. It says,

> Now the LORD had said unto Abram, "Get thee out of thy country, and from thy kindred, and from thy father's house, unto a land that I will show thee: And I will make of thee a great nation, and I will bless thee, and make thy name great; and thou shalt be a blessing: And I will bless them that bless thee, and curse him that curseth thee: and in thee shall all families of the earth be blessed."

Sin or unconfessed sin will set you back. It was through my getting away from my dysfunctional setting that I began to even realize that the situation I grew up in was dysfunctional. I went through Christian support groups for various dysfunctions. I even sought out a Christian psychologist. It was through my first marriage that I had my one and only child, Mark Anthony Porter Jr., born with the last name of *White* because his father and I were not married initially. I married at age eighteen, and he was nineteen. You see, the first time that I committed the sin of adultery, I did not just sin against my son's father. I sinned against my own body and God by committing adultery. I did violate his trust and our wedding vows and hurt him very deeply. I found out I was pregnant at age sixteen. I had never missed a menstrual cycle, and I knew that I had been sexually active on more than one occasion with my son's father, and I was scared, and I remembered that I did not want children.

My mom was in the basement doing laundry. We had moved up in the world, and we—my siblings and I—did not have to wash clothes in the bathtub any longer. Momma did not make us wash clothes in the bathtub; after coming home several times finding that we had washed clothes in the bathtub, she would make sure that she told us not to wash clothes in the bathtub, or we were going to get a whipping. I thought Momma did not mean that I would wash the clothes anyway. I found out Momma meant what she said.

So now we had a washer and dryer in the basement. My mom called me down to the basement, and she straight out asked me if I was pregnant. I told her I did not know and that I had a doctor's appointment set up for the following week. I have to give my mom credit. She had to be keeping a close eye on her children in order to know what was going on with me before I had even been to the doctor. My child's father knew I might be pregnant. I did not have to tell my mom anything. As I waited in the doctor's office for the test result, I was very scared what the result may be. I did not know anything about raising a child. When the medical staff came back, the test results were positive. My heart dropped.

My son's father was waiting on the playground in the back of my home, in the projects in North Minneapolis, for me to get home. He was very excited about me being pregnant. I did not understand why this was so exciting for him. I guess with him being his mother's only child, it was exciting for him to become a father. I was planning to have an abortion. My son's father talked me out of it with all of his excitement. I just could not have an abortion knowing how much he wanted our child. I am so glad I did not abort my baby in my womb. I just could not have an abortion knowing how much my child's father wanted our child. It did not take very much to change my mind about the abortion.

You see, I made a vow not to have children. You see, I was rejecting my son in the womb just as my mother did to me. I had to tell my son this story when he was sixteen because being dysfunctional myself at the time of the conception of our son, I was attracted to another dysfunctional person. And he told our son when he was sixteen that I was going to abort him. I had to quickly pray and tell him the truth. I told him, "Yes, I was going to abort you, but your dad changed my mind. I decided to keep you and raise you, and I love you and wanted you."

My son's father did this to hurt me not thinking about the pain it would cause our son. You see, hurt people hurt other people. (If you are hurting, seek professional godly counseling to get healed from your hurts.) "The LORD is longsuffering, and of great mercy, forgiving iniquity and transgression, and by no means clearing *the guilty,* visiting the iniquity of the fathers upon the children unto the third and fourth *generation*" (Numbers 14:18). This cycle was passed onto to me to reject my child in the womb. You see, I did not want to have any children, and Satan condemned me for some time after Mark's death with the statement "You were going to abort your son, and now he is dead." It was a vicious cycle, repeating itself. A cycle I feel that only a relationship with Jesus Christ can break.

I wanted to share this experience with you to show one way God was beginning to heal me. Now this was the fall of 1989, and I was thirty-one years old at this time. I have nothing against psychologists, but I had been seeing them since I was seventeen, and none of them were able to help me. It took the mighty hand of God to tell and show me why I was behaving like I was by cheating in relationships when I felt rejection. "But the Comforter, *which is* the Holy Ghost, whom the Father will send in my name, he shall teach you all things, and bring all things to your remembrance, whatsoever I have said unto you" (John 14:26). I now knew what was occurring with me. I could now pray for healing. I do not struggle with rejection any longer. It was a major breakthrough for me. It was like getting a diagnosis after a lengthy illness, and the Holy Spirit revealing to you what is wrong with you.

I wanted to share this to help someone else that may read my book. I am doing better at putting Christ first, but God is in the healing process with me.

> For I know that in me (that is, in my flesh,)
> dwelleth no good thing: for to will is present with
> me; but *how* to perform that which is good I find
> not. (Romans 7:18)

> Being confident of this very thing, that he
> which has begun a good work in you will perform
> *it* until the day of Jesus Christ. (Philippians 1:6)

It was through my relationship with Christ that God began to reveal things to me about myself. God would reveal things to me a little bit at a time for me to work on my character. I prayed for God to show me more, and he did. I wanted more revealed to me so that I could get myself together—like yesterday. I figured the more that God revealed to me, the quicker I could get myself straightened out, but the reality is that we will be working on ourselves until Jesus' second coming. I do not mean that you should be struggling in obvious sins such as fornication, adultery, or gossip, etc. God's word says in 1 Corinthians 10:13, "There hath no temptation taken you but such as is common to man: but God is faithful, who will not suffer you to be tempted above that ye are able; but will with temptation also make a way to escape, that ye may be able to bear it."

I got into professional Christian counseling, and it was during this time that my son Mark Jr., age sixteen at the time, asked, "Mom, why didn't you give me up for adoption?"

I had to quickly brace myself and pray and tell my son the truth. I told my son that I was going to have an abortion and, if it had not been for his father, I would have gone through with the abortion. I also told him I was sorry, and even though I wanted an abortion, I thank God that the abortion did not occur. I did change my decision, and I did love him and wanted him as my son now. I say to parents, "You don't tell your children things like this to hurt the other parent. You are hurting your children more."

It was at this point that we were in counseling to break the cycle of dysfunction, at least in my family with any grandchildren I may have had through my son, Mark Jr., but he did not understand the purpose of counseling, with him being a child at that time. He thought that in seeing a counselor, he would have someone to tell his mom to lighten up on the house rules and restrictions but to no avail. After realizing he was not going to get more freedom at home, Mark Jr. would not come home in time for our counseling appointments. So I discontinued the counseling at the counselor's advice.

A person must want to be helped. We cannot force help on them. Well, I never got the chance to break this vicious cycle of dysfunction with my grandchildren because my only child, Mark Jr., was taken from me two days before his nineteenth birthday in 1994. So I do not have any biological grandchildren. My life has not been the same without Mark. I struggled for two years with depression and not wanting to live. Twenty-seven years later, I still miss my son, but I am not grief-stricken like I was prior to my breakthrough in 2010. The breakthrough came after spending some time with my Heavenly Father in praise and worship when I received my breakthrough. After losing my son, I have felt such a great loss. It was no comparison to anything I have ever gone through. It is the kind of pain that violently rips a part of you away, unlike the willing and awaited birth and delivery of my child, which bought great joy into my life.

I would like to share my son's birth with you. I was sixteen going on seventeen. I did not know at all who God was making me to be. The night I went into labor, I could not sleep and used the bathroom quite frequently before I knew what was going on. I began to realize that I was having contractions about five minutes apart. I believe it was my oldest sister I called. I do not believe I called my mother's home. I knew she still had seven children living at home. My mom did get to the hospital eventually before the birth. I do not remember whether my sister or I telephoned her. I telephoned the Boy's Group Home where my son's father was living. He was not given the message until the next morning. He ran all the way to the hospital, and he was drenched in sweat when he reached the hospital.

I had to choose between my mom and my son's father who would be in the labor and delivery room with me. My mom appeared to be sad when I chose my son's father. I felt closeness with my son's father that I never felt with no one before. He had been very supporting, comforting, and loving throughout my pregnancy. I was not very nice to him through my contractions. Mark's father was very understanding as usual. There was a team of student doctors viewing the delivery through an observation window. They took advantage of me because of my age. My son was delivered on a Monday at 10:50 a.m. in the Hennepin County General Hospital in Minneapolis, Minnesota; and he came out crying. He did not have to be slapped. I felt no special feelings that I can remember. I was only glad to get the pregnancy over. When they placed him in my arms, me being young and uneducated about newborn babies, the first thing I thought was *Oh, what an ugly baby*. This was unusual for a mother. Just as when my son's body was cradled in his casket, this same mother at his second funeral having a sensitive nose as I do, I could smell my son's body decaying, and I was concerned about the attendees at the funeral being uncomfortable because of the odor.

I had my fourth marriage approximately two years after my son's death. Even before making the decision to remarry for the fourth time, I did some things that I am not proud to talk about. I was about three months in my third marriage when Mark Jr. died. I moved out on October 17, 1994, which was also the same day the young man who murdered my son was sentenced for my son's death. I had my third marriage annulled. I was unable to deal with my grief and problems in the marriage at the same time, so I moved out. If I had known better not to make any major decisions in your life when going through such grief or crisis, I would not have annulled my third marriage or gotten married for the fourth time. I committed adultery during this grief period while still legally married. I went through a variety of emotions. Even today, it is sometimes difficult for me to be around people with children, especially on holidays, mainly Christmas. I married my fourth husband to feel like I had family, only to be alienated by his daughter, and he kept his family away from me. This is why it is vitally important for us to have a close, intimate relationship with our Lord and Savior so we do not feel this loneliness.

My fourth husband was verbally, emotionally, and physically abusive. I believe he was trying hard to break my spirit, but to no avail. I had begun praying years before my son's death, that my son Mark would not die a violent death because of the illegal activity he was getting into. Mark died a violent death anyhow. I made all the wrong decisions, and I went through all this because I became angry with God, something I prayed I would never do. I told God that if Mark Jr. had to die, allow him to die from an illness because then, maybe I would have time to say goodbye. I do not have any idea why I would pray such a prayer. I now understand after not being able to be present when my mom took her last breath, I would not have been able to watch my son take his last breath.

God, my Heavenly Father, has nothing to do with premature death and murder. John 10:10 says, "The thief cometh but to steal, and to kill, and to destroy: I am come that they might have life, and that they might have life, and that they might have it more abundantly." This type of death is of the devil. I was over two thousand miles away when my son died. I wanted to be with him when he died. I wanted to be holding him in my arms as he walked through the valley of the shadow of death. I wanted to be there to say I loved him and I will miss him. I wanted to let him know that everything was going to be okay because our Lord and Savior would be there to welcome him into heaven. Second Corinthians 5:8 says, "We are confident, *I say*, and willing rather to be absent from the body, and to be present with the Lord."

I was unable to be there, and I still often wish I could have been there. Would it make my loss or pain any different? I do not think it would. God was there then, and he is here now, even when it feels as though I am all alone. My Heavenly Father knew best. When my mom was ill and the doctors had given her a death sentence, I was believing for healing for my mother to no avail. I told my Heavenly Father that if I did not have to be there when Mom passed, I would rather not be, but if he needed me to be there, I would be there. It was so painful watching my mother on her deathbed. I was believing God for a miracle. So God knew what he was doing when my son died; God knew I would not be able to manage the grief. I went home from my mother's hospital room after being there all night and into the afternoon in my mother's room to get some rest. It was snowing over the hospital that day and not in the area I was staying. It rained hard the day I buried my son. God, my heavenly Father, new I loved the rain. I heard later that mom loved the snow'; although I knew she did not like to be out in it. The snow was for me since it was too cold to get rain. If we have lived long enough, we know that everything does not go the way we want them to go. I believe God has a plan for my life, including using my son's death to help others.

It was through my last marriage that I finally decided to be obedient to God after marrying the third time, knowing that it was out of line with God's word and his rhema word to me, Sheila. I know I have been married four times. What I mean is that I was young when I married my son's father, and I did not have the understanding about God that I have now. I also believe in my heart that if I had stayed married, I should have stayed married to my son's father, my first marriage. I was also never told directly by God that I should not have married my son's father. So this is why I call the fourth marriage the third marriage. It was like each marriage got worse in stages. The fourth marriage was seven times worse than the other two. So at this point in my life, I told God I no longer want to do it Sheila's way but his way. I was tired of getting knocks and bruises. I stayed faithful to that marriage and remained celibate until two years later.

I still fall short of God's glory and fell into sexual sins in the next relationship after two years of celibacy. It was about this time I had to go to St. Louis for my grandfather's funeral. I met a man while in St. Louis, which is what I allowed to bring me to St. Louis and the fact that for nine years, I had wanted to live closer to my family who lived mostly in the Midwest area. I thank God he is a forgiving God, and I am not in habitual sin any longer. I began writing letters to this same man on my computer and sending them by fax. I met this man when I was in St. Louis for my grandfather's funeral. As I sat there in the church, I thought, *How sad it is that you have to wait to learn a lot about your grandfather as his obituary is read as his body lies in a casket.* I did not know my grandfather, Elmer Christopher White, very well. I do know that I always enjoyed his company. He nicknamed me Sheeiko. My grandfather was not as complicated to me as the women or females in my life. I felt relaxed around him. There always seemed to be competitiveness between the females in my family I did not like. I always got along fine with most of the males in my family.

After I went back to Sacramento, California, I began to connect with the person I met while in Saint Louis, Missouri, for my grandfather's funeral. A week after I had returned home, I made a decision to move back to my place of birth. The following month, we totally connected with each other, and we committed ourselves to a relationship with each other. So I have continued to send him faxes because he enjoyed receiving them. It was my writing the faxes to him that I would begin noticing the things I was writing, especially when I would pray for the Holy Spirit to anoint my fingers to write. It was in writing letters to this person through a fax that I began to really see that I had a special gift to write.

It was in the early part of 2019 that I had what I will call a spiritual awakening. I knew my son loved me; he was the one person on earth that I knew loved me. I had a series of relationships that did not work. After he died, I started attempting to create this family with men and their children. I had been doing this the twenty-six years that my son had been gone from this side of heaven. God my Father told me that I did not have to keep creating families with these men and their children to only to be rejected by them. He said I was a part of royalty, of a royal family. I did not have to create these families because I was a part of his family. God told me it was time to finish the book. I need to finish this instruction from God so that he can give me the next instruction.

Over the years, I just put myself in places I should not have been. I have learned better to protect my boundaries. I am sure this is why pastors teach unmarried persons today not to date. You only end up setting yourself up for a great fall. I was taught that when you have sex before marriage, you sow seeds of separation. So I have experienced this time and time again in relationship after relationship. There's so much damage and chaos that premarital sex can cause, and I will never allow my flesh to talk me into this again, but I did. What I needed was healing, not a relationship. I say to the unmarried, don't allow yourselves to be in this situation; it just causes tremendous pain for both parties. I try my best to do right by God. I went to a good Bible-teaching, Bible-believing church where they taught unmarried adults not to date and to wait for God to show you your mate. We are also taught to be doers of God's Word and not hearers only.

James 1:22 says, "But be ye doers of the word, and not hearers only, deceiving your own selves." I have also learned how to pray for exactly what I want in a mate as God and I prepare myself for my mate. I know God is able to prepare the damage I have allowed to happen in previous relationships. Romans 8:1 says, "*There is* therefore now no condemnation to them which are in Christ Jesus, who walk not after the flesh, but after the Spirit." Joel 2:25 says, "And I will restore to you the years that the locust hath eaten, the cankerworm, and the caterpillar, and the palmerworm, my great army which I sent among you." God did not have to pry my hands off this relationship that was not good. I finally broke loose. Do believe me; I will wait this time. I do not want someone else's husband; I want the man of God that God has for me.

Guess what, I did not wait. I became caught up with an individual that was controlling and a liar. It is obvious there is still healing for me to do. I was living with this person. The relationship was over early, but I was still living in his house in a separate room. I had already made the decision to move out. He managed to tear my right rotator cuff before I moved out. It was in the midst of my mess that my Heavenly Father told me that I was a part of his family, a part of royalty, and I did not need to create these families anymore, and it was in this same setting that my Heavenly Father told me that it was time to finish my book.

After being out of this abusive and unsafe situation and living in the lower level of someone's subbasement apartment, I had two dreams a week apart from each other about two different quality men. God told me that if I would wait, he has a quality man for me too. I told my Heavenly Father that I would wait. In the meantime, I choose to enjoy my times as an unmarried woman serving God.

I wanted to author this book, and a few others, to help someone else. Certain people have told me that I have a lot to share, and I would be a good writer. I also feel my writing is a gift from God. So as I write these pages, I ask the Holy Spirit to anoint my fingers to write. My prayer is that I hope that my book will help at least one person, and that she or he may go on to help hundreds maybe even thousands. I also pray that the person reading this book does not give up on life. Please take life in whatever increments you need to, rather it be a second or even a microsecond at a time, a minute at a time, a step at a time, or even a day at a time or an hour at a time. You must handle life in the amount you are able to handle it. God bless you.

That good success for me is marrying the man God has for me. I have married the man that I wanted four times, and I still do not have a husband. St. John 4:16–18 says,

> Jesus saith unto her, "Go, call thy husband, and come hither." The woman answered and

said, "I have no husband." Jesus said unto her, "Thou hast well said, 'I have no husband': For thou hast had five husbands; and he whom thou now hast is not thy husband: in that saidst thou truly."

As some of you know, we do not have a problem getting a spouse, but we do not know how to hold onto them. If you truly put your focus on God, and you make God your husband or wife, God will teach and prepare you to be a good spouse for your mate. You must wholeheartedly seek to be obedient to God's Word.

My Testimony

I will start with my testimony of being the common-law woman at the well. I live with a man for four years in the hopes that we would get married. It never happened. The person is still unmarried today, and I have gone on to marry three other men. I shared his bed. I shared the rent. I cooked his meals. I also shared in the expense of owning a home that was never mine. I did not start out sharing homeowner's expense. I did it in the hopes that the person would get out of the mindset of "It's mine. It's mine," and maybe begin thinking it's ours. It never happened. I moved on. I do not stick around when I am not happy. I just rebound to the next set of bad circumstances. I am now obeying God as a single woman. I do not think of any situation as wasted time. I believe God can use every situation for his good, and he is. I am writing about it. It was August 1998 when God's Holy Spirit gave me the title of this book and several chapter titles. I am writing the book now to get it published to be used of God to help someone else.

My book is unfolding as I walk this Christian walk, and God is anointing me to write. I can only share my life as I experienced and understood it as an individual. I know some of you may read this book and feel I am telling your story. God may have even told you to write this book, but you chose not to listen to God. God does not need us. We need him. If we do not do what God gives us specifically to do, God will just assign it to someone else. I believe you could author a book and hope you do share your story with someone else. I double dare you to trust God and step out on faith. You can do it. Yes, you can.

2

I Was the Samaritan Woman at the Well

There cometh a woman of Samaria to draw water:
Jesus saith unto her, "Give me to drink."

—St. John 4:7

You may ask me why I use the past tense in saying that I *was* the Samaritan woman at the well. You see, I am no longer at the well. I am now at Jesus' feet just as Mary was in Luke 10:39 where it says: "And she had a sister called Mary, which also sat at Jesus' feet, and heard his word." I once was cumbered about many things. I was cumbered about the obvious sin in my life. I had no peace. I was cumbered about the men in my life—yes, the men in my life. At times in my life, I had more than one man in my life. Maybe it was a boyfriend, a live-in situation, or even one of those four men that I had chosen to marry. I was not satisfied.

I know you have heard about the feeling of void, like something was missing in your life. I no longer feel that void. I have filled that void or the emptiness with God the Father, God the Son, and God the Holy Spirit. I accepted the Jesus Christ as my personal Lord and Savior. I spend time with him, God, daily. For me, being in God's presence is the greatest feeling of love I have never experienced and felt. I am not married now, but I believe I am not lacking any love. I am complete in God. God told me in 1 Corinthians 7:32b, "He that is unmarried careth for the things that belong to the Lord, how he may please the Lord."

I am quite happy serving my Lord and Savior. Yes, I desired to be married. My focus is seeking God's kingdom in all that I do. Matthew 6:33 says, "But seek ye first the kingdom of God, and his righteousness; and all these things shall be added unto you." When God is finished preparing me for the husband that he has for me, then I will get married. I will not worry when this will happen. I have enough to worry about in this day. "Take therefore no thought for the morrow: for the morrow shall take thought for the things of itself. Sufficient unto the day is the evil thereof" (Matthew 6:34). I believe what God's Word says about me. I was blessed to have been in a church that taught me on a regular basis about how to be a godly wife, what I needed to do before I get married, and what my responsibilities are as a wife. God loves me so much that he teaches me through the Holy Spirit and faithful men of God that teaches me the uncompromising word of God. I did it all wrong in the past. Right now in my unmarried state, I will focus and care about the things of the Lord. I am enjoying my unmarried state immensely. I will also enjoy my married state whenever that happens. The married life is a big responsibility, but once I get married, I will take total pleasure in being his helpmeet and pleasing the man of God whom God places in my life.

3

The Road to the Well

Enter ye in at the strait gate: for wide *is* the gate, and broad *is*
the way, that leadeth to destruction, and many there be which
go in thereat: Because strait *is* the gate, and narrow *is* the
way, which leadteh unto life, and few there be that find it.

—Matthew 7:13–14

As some of you have read in my book about my life, you may ask
yourself these questions: Why did I feel that I was the woman
at the well, and how did I get to this point? Well, I grew up in a dysfunctional home and was born out of wedlock. I was the second of
four born out of wedlock in my family. I did not grow up with a positive Christian father in my life. He was not there at all until my adult
life. Yes, I lived with him when I was in the ninth grade. Dad was not
present. I pursued a relationship with him. I feel that knowing what
I knew about the man my father was when he was alive, it probably
was to my benefit that he was not around. Through my relationship
with my mother, I learn to hug the people I loved. My father was not
a hugger. I am writing this from my experience and my perspective.

I was not raised in the church, but I thank God for my Big
Mamma, my dad's mother, who took me and my sister to church
when we were with her. I feel that she is the reason I have a personal
relationship with Jesus Christ today.

I can remember when I was twelve years old; I said I would never get married and that I didn't want any children. Ironically, I had one child and four husbands. I had two of those marriages annulled. You see, I was looking for love in the wrong places, just as my mother did. The love we need is always there, waiting with open arms: God the Father, God the Son, and God the Holy Spirit. There were four different biological fathers of my mother's children. Most of the time, it is a little girl's dream to get married and have children. I was not that little girl who wanted marriage and children. Maybe it was the turmoil and strife that I saw growing up in my mother's marriage that made me not want to get married. I could not say for sure. I was just a child seeing things through the eyes of a child. My mother married the last five children's father. The same thing could have occurred, even worse, to me, except God did not allow me to have a child with every man I had sex with. Thank God. You see I was repeating the cycle to the third and fourth generation (see Numbers 14:18). I was doing what my mom did and what some of my aunts did, as well as my grandmother with one of her children. I believe that only a personal relationship with Jesus Christ can break this cycle. I thank our Heavenly Father that he is a forgiving God.

At age sixteen and already having my first child, I had moved out and gotten my own apartment. I was an emancipated minor. It was at age seventeen that my mother called a family meeting to tell me and my other siblings that she was getting married to another female. It is funny to me that I do not remember any other family meetings. It sure would have been nice to have family meeting on a regular basis to learn about the birds and the bees. I was very angry at my mom because I felt my sisters and brothers still living at home would be ridiculed at school and by the neighborhood children about our mother's lifestyle. I was not expecting my mom to tell us she was getting married to another woman. Come on now, that is unnatural. I knew my mother's relationship with this woman was peculiar.

My mother was practicing the lifestyle of a lesbian female, and she was playing the male role. So you see, I did everything in my power to let people know I was not a lesbian. So on top of the generational curse, I had allowed Satan to put another curse upon me. I slept with numerous men to prove to myself and all those around me that I was not a lesbian. How could I be? I enjoyed men too much. It was those same men that hurt and betrayed me. So when you are not totally grounded in a relationship with God, you are bound to get off track—which I did more than I care to mention. I sinned repeatedly and habitually. It's just when you think you have it together, and God allows you to see you cannot do it without a daily relationship with him. I thank God for allowing me to see on a regular basis that I cannot do it without him.

When I look back at the different things that I have been through over the years, those are the times that helped me know today that I cannot do it without him. And as I write these pages in an attempt to readjust to my new living arrangements and relocation to Missouri, I see how much I need God in every situation of my readjustment to St. Louis, Missouri. I am now living in Minnesota where our mother moved us to from St. Louis, Missouri.

I hope and pray that I am in some way helping you to see what led me to being the woman at the well. For the young ladies and young men that may read my book, I pray you go the narrow road, that you wait for the mate God has for you. My advice to you is to find yourself a good Bible-teaching church that believes in living out Gods word. James 1:22 says, "But be ye doers of the word, and not hearers only, deceiving your own selves." Pair yourself up with an older Christian mentor of the same sex, someone you can trust and will be completely honest with you to be accountable. I know that accountability would have kept me out of many situations that I should not have been involved in. I have grown from those situations, those bad experiences. If I had it to do over again, I would choose accountability, but you know, we think we have it all together, and we do not want anyone in our business. What that really is, we do not want anyone in our business in case we decide we are going to fornicate or to knowingly commit sin.

Please believe me; I am growing each and every day. I intend to be a godly example to those around me from this day forward. I shall also allow my light to shine, and it is shining today. I am blessed and highly favored, walking in righteousness and empowered to prosper.

God absolutely loves me. He gave his only begotten son for you and me. John 3:16 says, "For God so loved the world, that he gave his only begotten Son, that whosoever believeth in him should not perish, but have everlasting life." I am no longer at the well.

4

Disobedience Will Not Take
You Far with God

Yea, all Israel have transgressed thy law, even by departing, that
they might not obey thy voice; therefore the curse is poured
upon us, and the oath that *is* written in the law of Moses
the servant of God, because we have sinned against him.

—Daniel 9:11

I knew all too well about disobedience to God's Word—not just
disobedience, repeated disobedience. I am in no way happy or
proud of my repeated disobedience. I know someone may be thinking, Well, God's word says in Romans 3:23, "For all have sinned and
come short of the Glory of God."

I was committing obvious sins, sexual sins. God's word says
in Hebrew 12:1, "Wherefore seeing we also are compassed about
with so great a cloud of witnesses, let us lay aside every weight, and
the sin which doth so easily beset *us*, and let us run with patience
the race that is set before us." Someone may be saying, "God is
a forgiving God." Romans 6:1, 2 says, "I say to you, 'What shall
we say then? Shall we continue in sin, that grace may abound?'
God forbid. How shall we, that are dead to sin, live any longer
therein?" What I believe this means is that we do not practice sin

habitually any longer. Romans 3:23, 24 says, "For all have sinned, and come short of the glory of God; Being justified freely by his grace through the redemption that is in Christ Jesus." None of us will be free from to sin until Jesus Christ's second coming. That is those that have accepted Jesus Christ as his or her personal savior. We may not be in obvious sin. We could just be in the sin of omission.

Yes, God is a forgiving God. God's word also says in 1 John 1:9, "If we confess our sins, he is faithful and just to forgive us *our* sins, and to cleanse us from all unrighteousness." Hebrew 8:12 says, "For I will be merciful to their unrighteousness, and their sins and their iniquities will I remember no more." I do feel that at some point, we must grow up and stop being baby Christians and begin to do whatever we can to be mature Christians. Whether that may take going to Sunday school, Bible study, and spending more time in private prayer, you must do what it takes. Our Lord God is a righteous God. Exodus 9:27 says, "And Pharaoh sent, and called for Moses and Aaron, and said unto them, I have sinned this time: the LORD *is* righteous, and my people *are* wicked." This was after the tenth plague of hail and fire.

Pharaoh had sinned against God several times earlier, and he continued to sin even after that even after the last plague; he continued to be disobedient unto God even after seeing all the plagues God did upon the Egyptians on behalf of and for the benefit of the children of Israel for them to trust God. Please read Exodus 9:22 through Exodus 15:5. It was God that hardened Pharaoh's heart from before the exodus of the children of Israel and during the exodus (Exodus 4:17–14:21). I believe God did it for the children of Israel to see the salvation of the Lord and for them to trust Him. We are just like the children of Israel. God has been our salvation repeatedly through healing our infirmities and blessing us financially, etc. He has blessed us with rent/mortgage money just before foreclosure. He has provided for us time after time. We are just like the children of Israel in the wilderness. We murmur, complain, doubt, and do not trust God. Like the Pharaoh, we sin habitually time and time again, but even with all of his sin, God used the situation for his glory and to show the children of Israel that they could trust him. I do believe that I would rather to be used by God because of obedience in my life and not from being disobedient.

I write these pages to let you know that you are not alone in your struggle with obvious sins. Rather that sin be gossiping, pride, adultery, drinking, smoking, going on the casino boats/buying lottery tickets, or fornication, I write because I want you to know at some point that we must trust God and be obedient to his Word. We have to live out God's Word in our lives.

You can choose to have a mediocre life or the abundant life, which Jesus Christ came to give us. John 10:10 says, "The thief cometh not, but for to steal, and to kill, and to destroy: I am come that they might have life, and that they might have it more abundantly." If you are out there half stepping, straddling the fence, and not living out the Word of God to the fullest, Satan does not care if you are a mediocre Christian. He will allow you to think you are living the good life. Take notice, I did not say the "abundant life." It is just like the dream I had one night where I was living in the projects, and I had gone out of town and returned to find my apartment had been broken into, ramshackle, and with things stolen. It left me feeling angry and violated. If you have confessed Jesus Christ as your personal Savior, you are violating the temple of God, your body. First Corinthians 6:18–20 says,

> Flee fornication. Every sin that a man doeth is without the body; but he that committeth fornication sinneth against his own body. What? know ye not that your body is the temple of the Holy Ghost which is in you, which ye have of God, and ye are not your own? For ye are bought with a price; therefore glorify God in your body, and in your spirit, which are God's.

When I say we, I include myself because I daily learn to obey and trust God. I learn to obey God not just in his written Word, the

Holy Bible, but his rhema word directly to me. God is not a man that he should lie.

> That by two immutable things, in which *it was* impossible for God to lie, we might have a strong consolation, who have fled for refuge to lay hold upon the hope set before us. (Hebrew 6:18)

> In hope of eternal life, which God, that cannot lie, promised before the world began. (Titus 1:2)

> Finally, my brethren, be strong in the Lord, and in the power of his might. Put on the whole armour of God, that ye may be able to stand against the wiles of the devil. For we wrestle not against flesh and blood, but against principalities, against powers, against the rulers of the darkness of this world, against spiritual wickedness in high *places*. Wherefore take unto you the whole armour of God, that ye may be able to withstand in the evil day, and having done all, to stand. Stand therefore, having your loins girt about with truth, and having on the breastplate of righteousness; And your feet shod with the preparation of the gospel of peace; Above all, taking the shield of faith, wherewith ye shall be able to quench all the fiery darts of the wicked. And take the helmet of salvation, and the sword of the Spirit, which is the word of God. Praying always with all prayer and supplication in the Spirit, and watching thereunto with all perseverance and supplication for all saints. (Ephesians 6:10–18)

We must remember to draw on God's strength to keep us out of sin and not our weak strength because soon you think you have some sin conquered, and here comes tall, dark, and handsome; and he sweeps you off your feet and you find out you do not have certain areas in your life conquered as you thought because, for example, I had been abstinent for two years when I fell again to sexual sins. God's grace is sufficient for you and me. So do not lose hope in being able to conquer the sin of fornication. Or any habitual sin. You will get tired of lying down with a man that is not your husband or a woman that is not your wife. That is Bible standards. Not the law of the land. God is able to keep us if we allow him. What I have learned is even though I am more than grown and well over eighteen and I live alone, there are just certain situations that I cannot personally allow myself to be in if I want to keep from falling into the same trap over and over again. We must always be watchful to watch out for Satan's tricks and devices because God's Word says in 1 Peter 5:8, "Be sober, be vigilant; because your adversary the devil, as a roaring lion, walketh about, seeking whom he may devour."

Satan is a father of lies. "Ye are of *your* father the devil, and the lusts of your father ye will do. He was a murderer from the beginning, and abode not in the truth, because there is no truth in him. When he speaketh a lie, he speaketh of his own: for he is a liar, and the father of it" (John 8:44). God's Word also says in James 4:7–8, "Submit yourselves therefore to God. Resist the devil, and he will flee from you. Draw nigh to God, and he will draw nigh to you. Cleanse your hands, *ye* sinners; and purify your hearts, *ye* double minded." We must believe what God's word says in James 1:6–8, "But let him ask in faith, nothing wavering. For he that wavereth is like a wave of the sea driven with the wind and tossed. For let not that man think that he shall receive any thing of the Lord. A double minded man *is* unstable in all his ways." And Mark 11:24 also says, "Therefore I say unto you, What things soever ye desire, when ye pray, believe that ye receive *them* and ye shall have them."

I had a $50,000 a year salary, and I felt like I could spend my money whenever and on whatever I wanted; plus, there was obvious sin in my life. I was not being a good steward over what God had blessed me with. I have struggled for years in obvious sins, and I have become the borrower and not the lender. Deuteronomy 28:44 says,

"He shall lend to thee, and thou shalt not lend to him: he shall be the head, and thou shalt be the tail." Please read Deuteronomy 28:1–14 where the scriptures tell you of your blessing for obeying the Lord your God this day.

I believe that in order to get the promises of God, we must have a daily walk of obedience. Despite my sins for several years, I was not practicing sins habitually. God did continue to bless me, but imagine the blessings I missed out on because of not having complete obedience in my life. I can track back to at least a couple of different times that God gave me chances to start fresh. I was allowed to pay off some bills completely in 1989. I sold a home, and I did not reinvest the money in another home. I suffer great capital-gains losses behind this decision. I should have at least put the amount I owed on taxes away for the capital gain. When we're not fully trusting in God, we follow the wrong voice. When God's Holy Spirit tells you to get all sin out of your life, you had better do it.

You may ask, "How do you know what sin?" Believe me, when God's Holy Spirit speaks to you, you will know what sin it is if you are honest with yourself. Back in 2000, in the Sunday morning service, I was told this very thing. There was a situation of sin trying to develop in my life that I did get rid of. It seems as though when you have sin under control, Satan will send another situation your way. Even Satan tempted Jesus in the wilderness, but Jesus did not sin. St. Luke 4:12–13 says, "And Jesus answering said unto him, 'It is said, Thou shalt not tempt the Lord thy God. And when the devil had ended all the temptation, he departed from him for a season.'" Satan leaves you for but a season, so you need to always be watchful because Satan is always lurking. First Peter 5:8 says, "Be sober, be vigilant, because your adversary the devil, as a roaring lion, walketh about, seeking whom he may devour." In my life, Satan will not just try to take out one Christian; he will involve two. We are not just affecting ourselves and the other Christian; there are our unsaved love ones that are counting on us to do the right thing.

Then there are those who want an excuse to continue in sin, and it will not take much. We are affecting our testimony by continuing in habitual sin. You see, our unsaved love ones and friends put us on a pedestal, and it should be Jesus they are looking to. They do not know any better. There are people watching our behavior, you could not even imagine. They see us going to Sunday services and other church services, then they see a male go into your home late at night and come out the next morning. God's word says in 1 Thessalonians 5:22, "Abstain from all appearance of evil." Who is going to listen to our testimony when our lives are no different than the unsaved or backsliders' lives?

I will give my own perfect example of how disobedience gets nowhere. I am now an older adult. I have gone from $25 an hour to $6.45–9.16 per hour. I have gone from buying property to renting someone else's property and dealing with the adjoining tenants' roaches and loud music. I have gone from being a police officer to being a safety officer. I have gone from having a little debt to having great debts. I have gone from living in California with a few great friends to having to make friends all over again and living in Missouri, a state with a slave mentality.

I have gone from a relationship of celibacy to a relationship where I find myself on occasions having sex with someone that there is a strong possibility he may not be my husband. I have gone from marriages with no commitment to boyfriend-and-girlfriend relationship with no commitment. I am having challenges with my finances. I am at the best place to be in order to learn to trust and see the salvation of God while I slowly and surely dig my way out of the financial bondage I have put myself in, and it is he who gives the power to get wealth (Deuteronomy 8:18).

I am learning patience through this dreaded temporary state. I learned to live frugal, as I should have when I had plenty. I thank God for the situation that I am in because with it comes valuable lessons. I am learning to trust God while I put my flesh under subjection. I have repented, and God will restore to me the years that the locust hast eaten, the cankerworm, and the caterpillar, and the palmerworm.

Joel 2:25 says, "And I will restore to you the years that the locust hath eaten, the cankerworm, and the caterpillar, and the palmerworm, my great army which I sent among you." I will be the lender and not the borrower. Being the lender comes with daily obedience. Deuteronomy 28:1–14 says,

> And it shall come to pass, if thou shalt hearken diligently unto the voice of the LORD thy God, to observe *and* to do all his commandments which I command thee this day, that the LORD thy God will set thee on high above all nations of the earth: And all these blessings shall come on thee, and overtake thee, if thou shalt hearken unto the voice of the LORD thy God. Blessed *shalt* thou *be* in the city, and blessed *shalt* thou *be* in the field. Blessed *shall be* the fruit of thy ground, and the fruit of thy cattle, the increase of the kine, and the flocks of thy sheep. Blessed *shall* be thy basket and thy store. Blessed *shalt* thou be when thou comest in, and blessed *shalt* thou be when thou goest out. The LORD shall cause thine enemies that rise up against thee to be smitten before thy face: they shall come out against thee one way, and flee before thee seven ways. The LORD shall command the blessing upon thee in thy storehouses, and in all that thou settest thine hand unto; and he shall bless thee in the land which the LORD thy God giveth thee. The LORD shall establish thee an holy people unto himself, as he hast sworn unto thee, if thou shalt keep the commandments of the LORD thy God, and walk in his ways. And all people of the earth shall see that thou art called by the name of the LORD; and they shall be afraid of thee. And the LORD shall make thee plenteous in goods, in the fruit of thy body, and in the fruit of thy cattle, and in the fruit of thy ground, in the land which the LORD sware unto thy fathers to give thee. The LORD shall open unto thee his good treasure, the heaven

to give the rain unto thy land in his season, and to bless all the work of thine hand: and thou shalt lend unto many nations, and thou shalt not borrow. And the LORD shall make thee the head, and not the tail; and thou shalt be above only, and thou shalt not be beneath; if that thou hearken unto the commandments of the LORD thy God, which I command thee this day, to observe and to do *them*: And thou shalt not go aside from any of the words which I command thee this day, *to* the right hand, or *to* the left, to go after other gods to serve them.

If you could, please read Deuteronomy 28:15–68 on the curses of disobedience. You do not want to go down this road. So at my older age, my disobedience has got me just where God said it would. Number 23:19 says, "God *is* not a man, that he should lie; neither the son of man, that he should repent: hath he said, and shall he not do *it*? or hath he spoken, and shall he not make it good?" Please do not feel like you have you have to experience everything in life before you learn to be obedient to God. I ask you to, please, learn from my mistakes.

5

Know Who You Are in Christ (Not through Your Children, Husband, or People)

Know Him for Yourself

Therefore if any man *be* in Christ, *he is* a new creature: old things are passed away; behold, all things are become new.

—2 Corinthians 5:17

It is very important that you know who you are in Christ because if you are not sure who you are in Christ, the storms of life will come. You have to be standing on a firm foundation of the Word of God. You have to know who the Bible says you are. You must know that you are predestined. "For whom he did foreknow, he also did predestinate *to be* conformed to the image of his Son, that he might be the firstborn among many brethren" (Romans 8:29). You must know that God knew you in your mother's womb.

Blessed *be* the God and Father of our Lord Jesus Christ, who hath blessed us with all spiritual blessings in heavenly *places* in Christ: According as he hath chosen us in him before the foundation of the world, that we should be holy and without blame before him in love: Having predestinated us unto the adoption of children by Jesus Christ to himself, according to the good pleasure of his will, To the praise of the glory of his grace, wherein he hath made us accepted in the beloved. In whom we have redemption through his blood, the forgiveness of sins, according to the riches of his grace; Wherein he hath abounded toward us in all wisdom and prudence; Having made known unto us the mystery of his will, according to his good pleasure which he hath purposed in himself: That in the dispensation of the fulness of times he might gather together in one all things in Christ, both which are in heaven, and which are on earth; *even* in him: In whom also we have obtained an inheritance, being predestinated according to the purpose of him who worketh all things after the counsel of his own will: That we should be to the praise of his glory, who first trusted in Christ. In whom ye also *trusted*, after that ye heard the word of truth, the gospel of your salvation: in whom also after that ye believed, ye were sealed with that holy Spirit of promise, Which is the earnest of our inheritance until the redemption of the purchased possession, unto the praise of his glory. (Ephesians 1:3–14)

You must know that God knew you in your mother's womb.

For thou hast possessed my reins: thou hast covered me in my mother's womb. I will praise thee; for I am fearfully *and* wonderfully made: marvellous *are* thy works; *and that* my soul knoweth right well. My substance was not hid from thee, when I was made in secret, *and* curiously wrought in the lowest parts of the earth.

> Thine eyes did see my substance, yet being unperfect; and in thy book all *my members* were written, *which* in continuance were fashioned, when *as yet there was* none of them. (Psalm 139:13–16)

You have to know that God has a plan and purpose for your life. "For I know the thoughts that I think, toward you, saith the LORD, thoughts of peace, and not of evil, to give you an expected end" (Jeremiah 29:11). You have to know that God the Father has a plan and a purpose for your life. You must be willing to stand on the firm foundation of God's Holy Word because the enemy will send people and situations your way to distract you from the things of God and pull you away from your purpose.

> The thief cometh not, but for to steal, and to kill, and to destroy: I am come that they might have life, and that they might have *it* more abundantly. (John 10:10)

> Casting all your care upon him; for he careth for you. Be sober, be vigilant; because your adversary the devil, as a roaring lion, walketh about, seeking whom he may devour: Whom resist stedfast in the faith, knowing that the same afflictions are accomplished in your brethren that are in the world. (1 Peter 5:7–8)

You have to be willing to do what it says in 2 Corinthians 10:3–6:

> For though we walk in the flesh, we do not war after the flesh: (For the weapons of our warfare *are* not carnal, but mighty through God to the pulling down of strong holds;) Casting down imaginations, and every high thing that exalted

itself against the knowledge of God, and bringing into captivity every thought to the obedience of Christ; And having in a readiness to revenge all disobedience, when your obedience is fulfilled.

People with well intentions will attempt to pull you in the directions of other religions; but if you have a firm relationship with the Godhead, that is, God the Father, God the Son, and God the Holy Spirit, you must have come by way of Jesus Christ.

> Jesus saith unto him, I am the way, the truth, and the life: no man cometh unto the Father, but by me. If ye had known me, ye should have known my Father also: and from henceforth ye know him, and have seen him. Philip saith unto him, Lord, show us the Father, and it sufficeth us. Jesus saith unto him, Have I been so long time with you, and yet hast thou not known me, Philip? he that hath seen me hath seen the Father; and how sayest thou then, Show us the Father? Believest thou not that I am in the Father, and the Father in me? the words that I speak unto you I speak not of myself: but the Father that dwelleth in me, he doeth the works. Believe me that I *am* in the Father, and the Father in me: or else believe me for the very works' sake. (John 14:6–11)

If you did not come to God the Father by accepting his Son Jesus Christ, then you and I do not serve the same God. You must have a relationship with Jesus Christ. Just like when you meet your future spouse, you have to spend time with them in order to get to know them. It is a lifetime commitment.

You want to get rooted and grounded in the Word of God so much so that when trials and tribulations come, you will have so marinated your spirit, soul, and body in the Word of God, that not anyone or anything can pull you away. You do not want to wait until you have a crisis in your family. You want to have the word hid in your heart. "Thy word have I hid in mine heart, that I might not sin against thee" (Psalm 119:11). You want to know God the Father, God the Son, and God the Holy Spirit. You want to meditate on God's Word day and night. Even if you do not have your Bible in front of you, you want to know the Word of God so much so that you can pull it up in your memory and meditate on it. We were created in their image. "And God said, Let us make man in our image, after our likeness: and let them have dominion over the fish of the sea, and over the fowl of the air, and over the cattle, and over all the earth, and over every creeping thing that creepeth upon the earth" (Genesis 1:26). We have that same speaking ability to speak what we want to see happen in our lives as long as it does not go against the Word of God. This is why it is vital that we renew our mind as it says in Romans 12:2, "And be not conformed to this world: but be ye transformed by the renewing of your mind, that ye may prove what *is* that good, and acceptable, and perfect, will of God." We must meditate on the Word of God so that we see ourselves with the things we believe are to happen in our lives. When God created the world, he saw it first. Do you remember how you used to use your imagination when you were little boys and girls? The Bible talks about childlike faith. Just like when your children believe there is nothing Mom and Dad cannot do. We need to get back to using our imaginations in a godly way. Set time aside daily to see the things you want to see happening in your life.

God is your Heavenly Father, and he was your Heavenly Father first before you had a natural father.

> And call no *man* your father upon the
> earth: for one is your Father, which is in heaven.
> (Matthew 23:9)

> But I say unto you, Love your enemies,
> bless them that curse you, do good to them that
> hate you, and pray for them which despitefully

use you, and persecute you; That ye may be the children of your Father which is in heaven: for he maketh his sun to rise on the evil and on the good, and sendeth rain on the just and on the unjust. For if ye love them which love you, what reward have ye? do not even the publicans the same?

And if ye salute your brethren only, what do ye more *than others*? do not even the publicans so? Be ye therefore perfect, even as your Father which is in heaven is perfect. (Matthew 5:44–48)

Jesus is the son of God. He was sent to be our savior the perfect sacrifice because his Father so love the world that he gave.

For God so loved the world, that he gave his only begotten Son, that whosoever believeth in him should not perish, but have everlasting life. (John 3:16)

Therefore the Lord himself shall give you a sign; Behold, a virgin shall conceive, and bear a son, and shall call his name Immanuel. (Isaiah 7:14)

Jesus was our perfect sacrifice born of a virgin who had not known a man sexually when Jesus was conceived in her womb.

After Jesus finished his ministry here on earth, he sent us the Holy Spirit.

And I will pray the Father, and he shall give you another Comforter, that he may abide with you forever; *Even* the Spirit of truth; whom the world cannot receive, because it seeth him not, neither knoweth him: but ye know him; for he dwelleth with you, and shall be in you. I will not leave you comfortless: I will come to you. (John 14:16–18)

But the Comforter, *which is* the Holy Ghost, whom the Father will send in my name, he shall teach you all things, and bring all things to your remembrance, whatsoever I have said unto you. (John 14:26)

And, behold, I send the promise of my Father upon you: but tarry ye in the city of Jerusalem, until ye be endues with power from on high. And he led them out as far as to Bethany, and he lifted up his hands, and blessed them. And it came to pass, while he blessed them, he was parted from them, and carried up into heaven. And they worshipped him, and returned to Jerusalem with great joy:
And were continually in the temple, praising and blessing God. Amen. (Luke 24:49–53)

The former treatise have I made, O Theophilus, of all that Jesus began both to do and teach, Until the day in which he was taken up, after that he through the Holy Ghost had given commandments unto the apostles whom he had chosen: To whom also he shewed himself alive after his passion by many infallible proofs, being seen of them forty days, and speaking of the things pertaining to the kingdom of God: And, being assembled together with *them*, commanded them that they should not depart from Jerusalem, but wait for the promise of the Father, which, *saith he*, ye have heard of me. For John truly baptized with water; but ye shall be baptized with the Holy Ghost not many days hence.

When they therefore were come together, they asked of him, saying, Lord, wilt thou at this time restore again the kingdom to Israel? And he said unto them, It is not for you to know the times or the seasons, which the Father hath put in his own power. But ye shall receive power, after that the Holy Ghost is come upon you: and ye shall be witnesses unto me both in Jerusalem, and in all Judaea, and in Samaria, and unto the uttermost part of the earth. And when he had spoken these things, while they beheld, he was taken up; and a cloud received him out of their sight. And while they looked stedfastly toward heaven as he went up, behold, two men stood by them in white apparel; Which also said, Ye men of Galilee, why stand ye gazing up into heaven? This same Jesus, which is taken up from you into heaven, shall so come in like manner as ye have seen him go into heaven. Then returned they unto Jerusalem from the mount called Olivet, which is from Jerusalem a sabbath day's journey. And when they were come in, they went up into an upper room, where abode both Peter, and James, and John, and Andrew, Philip, and Thomas, Bartholomew, and Matthew, James *the son* of Alphaeus, and Simon Zelotes, and Judas *the brother* of James. These all continued with one accord in prayer and supplication, with the women, and Mary the mother of Jesus, and with his brethren. (Acts 1:1–14)

And when the day of Pentecost was fully come, they were all with one accord in one place. And suddenly there came a sound from heaven as of a rushing mighty wind, and it filled all the house where they were sitting. And there appeared unto them cloven tongues like as of fire, and it sat upon each of them. And they were all filled with the Holy Ghost, and began to speak with other tongues, as the Spirit gave them utterance. (Acts 2:1–4)

Jesus kept is promise in sending the comforter, the Holy Spirit.

But the Comforter, *which is* the Holy Ghost, whom the Father will send in my name, he shall teach you all things, and bring all things to your remembrance, whatsoever I have said unto you. (John 14:26)

But ye have an unction from the Holy One, and ye know all things. I have not written unto you because ye know not the truth, but because ye know it, and that no lie is of the truth. Who is a liar but he that denieth that Jesus is the Christ? He is antichrist, that denieth the Father and the Son. Whosoever denieth the Son, the same hath not the Father: *[but]he that acknowledgeth the Son hath the Father also.* Let that therefore abide in you, which ye have heard from the beginning. If that which ye have heard from the beginning shall remain in you, ye also shall continue in the Son, and in the Father. And this is the promise that he hath promised us, *even* eternal life.

These *things* have I written unto you concerning them that seduce you. But the anointing which ye have received of him abideth in you, and ye need not that any man teach you: but as the same anointing teacheth you of all things, and is truth, and is no lie, and even as it hath taught you, ye shall abide in him. And now, little children, abide in him; that, when he shall appear, we may have confidence, and not be ashamed before him at his coming. If ye know that he is righteous, ye know that every one that doeth righteousness is born of him. (1 John 2:20–29)

You must know your Word, the stories in the Bible about God the Father, God the Son, and God the Holy Spirit the characters in the Bible so that you will be able to apply the Bible to your own circumstances. "And be not conformed to this world: but be ye transformed by the renewing of your mind, that ye may prove what *is* that good, and acceptable, and perfect will of God" (Romans 12:2). We are bombarded daily with the things of the world through social media, television, media, coworkers, family, and the news. We have to make a personal commitment to stay in the Word of God, the Bible to know God's will for our lives.

That if thou shalt confess with thy mouth the Lord Jesus, and shalt believe in thine heart that God hath raised him from the dead, thou shalt be saved. For with the heart man believeth unto righteousness; and with the mouth confession is made unto salvation. For the scripture saith, Whosoever believeth on him shall not be ashamed. For there is no difference between the Jew and the Greek: for the same Lord over all is rich unto all that call upon him. For whosoever shall call upon the name of the LORD shall be saved. How then shall they call on him in whom they have not believed? and how shall they believe in him of whom they have not heard? and how shall they hear without a preacher? And how shall they preach, except they be sent? as it is written, How beautiful are the feet of them that preach the gospel of peace, and bring glad tidings of good things! But they have not all obeyed the gospel. For Esaias saith, LORD, who hath believed

our report. So then faith *cometh* by hearing, and
hearing by the word of God. (Roman 10:9–17)

We have got to be in the Word of God so much so that we are able to imagine having every promise that we desire. We have to see the promises of God in our imagination. If you can see yourself with it in your imagination, you can have every promise. For example, I just got a hold of this revelation. I have taken time out daily using my imagination to see myself healed, in good relationships, blessed to be a blessing, and seeing myself at my book signing.

Beloved, I wish above all things that thou
mayest prosper and be in health, even as thy soul
prospereth. (3 John 2)

Let them shout for joy, and be glad, that
favour my righteous cause: yea, let them say continually, Let the LORD be magnified, which hath
pleasure in the prosperity of his servant. (Psalm
35:27)

The Godhead—that is, God the Father, God the Son, and God the Holy Spirit—wants us to prosper.

6

Through You, Other People Will Be Saved

And many of the Samaritans of that city believed on him for the saying of the woman, which testified, He told me all that ever I did. (John 4:39)

Who shall tell thee words, whereby thou and all thy house shall be saved. (Acts 11:14)

Jesus saith unto her, I that speak unto thee am *he*. And upon this came his disciples, and marvelled that he talked with the woman: yet no man said, What seekest thou? or, Why talkest thou with her? The woman then left her water-pot, and went her way into the city, and saith to the men, Come, see a man, which told me all things that ever I did: is not this the Christ? Then they went out of the city, and came unto him. In the mean while his disciples prayed him, saying, Master, eat. But he said unto them, I have meat to eat that ye know not of. Therefore said the disciples one to another, Hath any man brought him *ought* to eat? Jesus saith unto them, My meat is to do the will of him that sent me, and to finish his work. Say not ye, There are yet four months, and *then* cometh harvest? behold, I say unto you, Lift up your eyes, and look on the fields; for they are white already to harvest. And he that reapeth receiveth wages, and gathereth fruit unto life eternal: that both he that soweth and he that reapeth may rejoice together. And herein is that saying true, One soweth, and another reapeth. I sent you to reap that whereon ye bestowed no labour: other men laboured, and ye are entered into their labours. And many of the Samaritans of that city believed on him for the saying of the woman, which testified, He told me all that ever I did. So when the Samaritans were come unto him, they besought him that he would tarry with them: and he abode there two days. And many more believed because of his own word; And said unto the woman, Now we believe, not because of thy saying: for we have heard *him* ourselves, and know that this is indeed the Christ, the Saviour of the world. (John 4:26–42)

And the apostles and brethren that were in Judaea heard that the Gentiles had also received the word of God. And when Peter was come up to Jerusalem, they that were of the circumcision contended with him, Saying, Thou wentest in to men uncircumcised, and didst eat with them. But Peter rehearsed *the matter* from the beginning, and expounded it by order unto them, saying, I was in the city of Joppa praying: and in a trance I saw a vision, A certain vessel descend, as it had been a great sheet, let down from heaven by four corners; and it came even to me: Upon the which when I had fastened mine eyes, I considered, and saw fourfooted beasts of the earth, and wild beasts, and creeping things, and fowls of the air. And I heard a voice saying unto me, Arise, Peter; slay and eat. But I said, Not so, Lord: for nothing common or unclean hath at any time entered into my mouth. But the voice answered me again from heaven, What God hath cleansed, *that* call not thou common. And this was done three times: and all were drawn up again into heaven. And, behold, immediately there were three men already come unto the house where I was, sent from Caesarea unto me. And the Spirit bade me go with them, nothing doubting. Moreover these six brethren accompanied me, and we entered into the man's house: And he shewed us how he had seen an angel in his house, which stood and said unto him, Send men to Joppa, and call for Simon, whose surname is Peter; Who shall tell thee words, whereby thou and all thy house shall be saved. (Acts 11:1–14)

If you have lived God's word out in your life and before men, someone may just want to serve the God of the Bible you serve. That is God the Father, God the Son, and God the Holy Spirit. We have to be different than those around us. "Enter ye in at the strait gate: for wide *is* the gate, and broad *is* the way, that leadeth to destruction, and many there be which go in thereat: Because strait *is* the gate, and narrow *is* the way, which leadeth unto life, and few there be that find it" (Matthew 7:13–14). We have to set a godly example at home, school, work, and in the marketplace.

We cannot do things the way the world does. We have to be willing to say that we apologize when others will not. We must be willing to forgive when others won't. "For if ye forgive men their trespasses, your heavenly Father will also forgive you: But if ye forgive not men their trespasses, neither will your Father forgive your trespasses" (Matthew 6:14–15). We have to be the ones to set up a godly atmosphere in our environment. We have to do things the way

Jesus would have done them when he walked on the earth. "Behold, a virgin shall be with child, and shall bring forth a son, and they shall call his name Emmanuel, which being interpreted is, God with us" (Matthew 1:23). We just never know whether the person we are influencing in a godly way whether they will be the next Billy Graham. You are able to reach people in your sphere of influence that I may never reach and vice versa.

7

Speak the Word Only

The centurion answered and said, Lord, I am not worthy
that thou shouldest come under my roof: but speak
the word only, and my servant shall be healed.

—Matthew 8:8

If we would be like Jesus and only do like our Heavenly Father
says for us to say or do, I believe our lives would be so much more
fulfilled.

> Then answered Jesus and said unto them,
> Verily, verily, I say unto you, The Son can do
> nothing of himself, but what he seeth the Father
> do: for what things soever he doeth, these also
> doeth the Son likewise. (John 5:19)

> For I have not spoken of myself; but the
> Father which sent me, he gave me a command-
> ment, what I should say, and what I should speak.
> (John 12:49)

If we would simply ask ourselves what or how would my
Heavenly Father want me to act in this situation, or we would take

time to compose our words in our heart first, we all would have better outcomes. We may need to ask our Heavenly Father, "Daddy, please forgive me for the way that I handled a situation or my behavior." Sometimes we just have to take the effort to go back and say, "I apologize for our words or our actions." It is easier just to be right and do right the first time. I would suggest that you make time to adjust your attitude before you even leave your house. Spend some time in prayer for your job, coworkers, family, and situations you may encounter. Pray that you handle every situation the way Daddy would have you to handle them TTTS and P: "Take time to stop and pray."

8

Test and See the Salvation of the Lord

Beloved, believe not every spirit, but try the
spirits whether they are of God; because many
false prophets are gone out into the world.

—1 John 4:1

As I write this book and walk my daily life, its pages unfold as God's Holy Spirit anoints my hands to write. God is putting people in my path daily to provide encouragement, insight, direction, and contacts. God told me to trust him, and from this day forward, I will be trusting God where this book is concerned and take a daily step toward, trusting him completely in every other area of my life. Let's watch and see how God works through me to get the book he wants written published.

John 15:5 says, "I am the vine, ye *are* the branches: He that abideth in me, and I in him, the same bringeth forth much fruit: for without me ye can do nothing." Philippians 4:13 says, "I can do all things through Christ which strengtheneth me." Not only do I need to test and see the salvation of the Lord, I have to walk the walk of my daily confessions of faith that I had been confessing daily and that I said I believed. For instance, I had been saying a daily confession of faith that I believed I am a gifted writer, and everything I write will be published, and I will be paid for it abundantly for the furtherance of the Gospel and to get out of debt in Jesus' name. So you see, I believe I had to begin to walk in what I was confessing. I will give you an example of what I am saying. If I, Sheila, believe my book to be a bestseller and a commandment from God to write it, I had to work on my book every day like it was a business, just as the nine-to-five job I went to every day.

The good thing about writing is that it is something that I learned that I enjoyed immensely. So I wrote what I needed monetarily from God for the month and what I need to get out of debt because I was also believing a daily confession of faith saying, "Father, I thank you. I believe I am debt-free and that every need is met and every bill is paid off in Jesus' name." Now some of you may be thinking God expects us to do some things for ourselves, but I was working, plus I had a second job and was trying to get a third job, but after meeting with an already published author, I received an abundance of encouragement from her to trust in the Lord. I decided I would begin to step out on faith and begin to walk in what I was confession daily and to walk in it regardless of what people were saying or what it looked like. Second Corinthians 5:7 says, "For we walk by faith, not by sight. James 1:8 says A double minded man *is* unstable in all his ways." So I either believe God, or I do not. I cannot have it both ways. So watch me complete this book through Jesus Christ and watch God make this my first published work be a bestseller.

9

The Common-Law Wife at the Well

For thou hast had five husbands; and he whom thou now
has is not thy husband: in that saidst thou truly.

—John 4:18

I did not want to leave out the women who have lived with a man as her husband. The common-law wife had been what I would call it counterfeit. It has all the characteristics of a real marriage, but in the eyes of God, we were just committing fornication and, in some situations, even committing adultery. Why do we bother to give ourselves to men that are not even our husbands? God created sex and intended it for marriage. Hebrew 13:4 says, "Marriage is honourable in all, and the bed undefiled: but whoremongers and adulterers God will judge." We get right down and dirty with someone we may never even marry. I say to the common-law wife or common-law husbands, you are playing house. Not only are they literally not our spouse, they may be legally and naturally married to someone else.

Spiritually, God is preparing that individual for someone else, and it is more than likely it is not you. You are stopping their growth by shacking with him or her. God says, "Sex is beautiful inside marriage with your own spouse." "Marriage is honorable in all and the bed undefiled: but whoremongers and adulterers God will judge" (Hebrews 13:4). So if you are out there with someone

54

else's husband or wife with a man or woman that's not your spouse, let the situation go and repent. Do not believe the lie from the man or woman he/she is going to leave their wife or husband. Why would you want someone else's spouse? God has a mate tailor-made just for us.

Let us say that the individual leaves their spouse and marries you. What makes you think or believe that they are not going to leave you for someone else? God's word says in says in Galatians 6:7, "Be not deceived; God is not mocked; for whatsoever a man soweth, that shall he also reap." For those of you that are just doing patting and touching and masturbating with the opposite sex or the same sex and you are not penetrating each other, let me ask you a question: Can you say that the person you are touching inappropriately, that the both of you are not committing sin in the eyes of God. Matthew 5:28 says, "But I say unto you, That whosoever looketh on a woman to lust after her hath committed adultery with her already in his heart. First Thessalonians 5:22 says, "Abstain from all appearance of evil." Masturbating is opening the door to incubus and succubus, an evil spirit into your soul.

Allow me to ask you another question: Would you do what you're doing in front of another Christian whose opinion and moral character you value? If the answer is no, you may or should want to repent this very moment and do an about-face. First John 1:9 says, "If we confess our sins, he is faithful and just to forgive us *our* sins and to cleanse us from all unrighteousness." And if you have never been saved, Romans 10:9–10 says, "That if thou salt confess with thy mouth the Lord Jesus, and shalt believe in thine heart that God hath raised him from the dead, thou shalt be saved. For with the heart man believeth unto righteousness; and with the mouth confession is made unto salvation." Men, I do realize that maybe some of you wanted to truly get married, but your common-law wife chose not to marry you. I also realize that at some point, we made a choice to move in with a man and be unmarried, hoping that it would lead to marriage and it did not. Ladies, let us be real. Why would they marry you when they have all the comforts of marriage without the commitment? Ladies, we do have a choice. The choice is to accept Jesus

Christ as our personal savior and live a Christian life and wait for the mate God has for us.

For those of you who are a single Christian woman waiting and trusting God, what are you doing while you are waiting to prepare yourself for the husband God is preparing for you? Are you learning of God by studying and spending quiet time with him? Are you taking the counsel of God directly from his word?

> Now concerning virgins I have no commandment of the Lord: yet I give my judgment, as one that hath obtained mercy of the Lord to be faithful. I suppose therefore that this is good for the present distress, I *say* that *it is* good for a man so to be. Art thou bound unto a wife? seek not to be loosed. Art thou loosed from a wife? seek not a wife. But and if thou marry, thou hast not sinned; and if a virgin marry, she hath not sinned. Nevertheless such shall have trouble in the flesh. But I spare you. But this I say, brethren, the time *is* short; it remaineth, that both they that have wives be as though they had none; And they that weep, as though they wept not; and they that rejoice, as though they rejoiced not; and they that buy, as though they possessed not; And they that use this world, as not abusing it: for the fashion of this world passeth away. But I would have you without carefulness. He that is unmarried careth for the things that belong to the Lord, how he may please the Lord: But he that is married careth for the things that are of the world, how he may please *his* wife. There is difference *also* between a wife and a virgin. The unmarried woman careth for the things of the Lord, that she may be holy both in body and in spirit: but she that is married careth for the things of the world,

how she may please *her* husband. (1 Corinthians 7:25–32)

Are you meditating on God's Word day and night as it says in Joshua 1:8:

> This book of the law shall not depart out of thy mouth; but thou shall meditate therein day and night, that thou may observe to do according to all that is written therein: for then thou shalt make thy way prosperous, and then thou shalt have good success.

> Study to shew thyself approved unto God, a workman that needeth not to be ashamed, rightly dividing the word of truth. (2 Timothy 2:15)

That good success for me is marrying the man God has for me. I have married the man that I wanted four times, and I still do not have a husband. John 4:16–18 says,

> Jesus saith unto her, Go, call thy husband, and come hither. The woman answered and said, I have no husband. Jesus said unto her, Thou hast well said, I have no husband: For thou hast had five husbands; and he whom thou now hast is not thy husband: in that saidst thou truly.

I was so dysfunctional and so broken all the time that I was married. I tried to explain it to the first man I was married to, but he did not understand that I should not have been married to anyone or in a relationship with anyone. I told him the truth, but he was not ready to hear the truth that was my truth. I have not been married since 1998, and my Heavenly Father promised me in a dream I had in the early 1990s that he was going to make me whole, and with every step that I take he has been doing that for me. I am excited about what God is doing in my life. My heart is so happy. Thank you, Heavenly Father.

As some of you know, we do not have a problem getting a spouse, but we do not know how to hold onto them. If you truly put your focus on God, and you make God your husband or wife, God will teach and prepare you to be a good spouse for your mate. You must wholeheartedly seek to be obedient to God's word.

10

Women of the Bible Used by God

Then Peter opened *his* mouth, and said, Of a truth
I perceive that God is no respecter of persons;
But in every nation he that feareth him, and
worketh righteousness, is accepted with him.

—Acts 10:34–35

The reason I wanted to write this chapter is to encourage women from every age group and ethnic group. I have seen women from every age be victimized from their house to God's house. You may say that men have been abused also. I'm not disagreeing with you. Someone else should write that book. I am a woman, and I can only write from a woman's perspective. In the Bible, from Genesis to Revelation, women are mentioned and used for good or evil. I want to encourage you from this day forward not to allow yourself to be used for evil. "The LORD hath made all *things* for himself: yea, even the wicked for the day of evil" (Proverbs 16:4). As you read this chapter about the woman of the Bible used by God, choose to be a woman used by God for good. I will write about some of the women in the Bible that did evil to remind you not to be one of those that did evil.

The eyes of the LORD *are* upon the righteous, and his ears *are* open unto their cry. The face of the LORD is against them that do evil, to cut off the remembrance of them from the earth. *The righteous* cry, and the LORD heareth, and delivereth them out of all their troubles. The LORD *is* nigh unto them that are of a broken heart; and saveth such as be of a contrite spirit. Many *are* the afflictions of the righteous: but the LORD delivereth him out of them all.

He keepeth all his bones: not one of them is broken. Evil shall slay the wicked: and they that hate the righteous shall be desolate. The LORD redeemeth the soul of his servants: and none of them that trust in him shall be desolate. (Psalm 34:15–22)

Please read the whole chapter of Psalm 34. Now keep in mind that as I share about some of the stories of the women in the Bible, I may not write about them in the order that they appear in the Bible. I will just mention a few to make the point to encourage women of today.

Eve, the Mother of All Living

Starting with Genesis in the beginning, we have Eve, the mother all living. "And God said, Let us make man in our image, after our likeness: and let them have dominion over the fish of the sea, and over the fowl of the air, and over the cattle, and over all the earth, and over every creeping thing that creepeth upon the earth" (Genesis 1:26). We were made in the image of God just as man because we were taken out of the man. Genesis 1:28 says, "And God blessed them, and God said unto them, be fruitful, and multiply, and replenish the earth and subdue it: and have dominion over the fish of the sea, and over the fowl of the air, and over every living thing that moveth upon the earth."

And the LORD God took the man, and put him into the garden of Eden to dress it and to keep it. And the LORD God commanded the man, saying, Of every tree of the garden thou mayest freely eat: But of the tree of the knowledge of good and evil, thou shalt not eat of it: for in the day that thou eatest thereof thou shalt surely die. And the LORD God said, *It is* not good that the man should be alone; I will make him a help meet for him. And out of the ground the LORD God formed every beast of the field, and every fowl of the air; and brought *them* unto Adam to see what he would call them: and whatsoever Adam called every living creature, that *was* the name thereof. And Adam gave names to all cattle, and to the fowl of the air, and to every beast of the field; but for Adam there was not found an help meet for him. And the LORD God caused a deep sleep to fall upon Adam, and he slept: and he took one of his ribs, and closed up the flesh instead thereof; And the rib, which the LORD God had taken from man, made he a woman, and brought her unto the man. And Adam said, This *is* now bone of my bones, and flesh of my flesh: she shall be called Woman, because she was taken out of Man. Therefore shall a man leave his father and his mother, and shall cleave unto his wife: and they shall be one flesh. And they were both naked, the man and his wife, and were not ashamed. (Genesis 2:15–25)

Our Heavenly Father took us out of man and brought us to him. God created man and woman to be together to birth children into the world, and no law that man has set in place is going the supersede God's law.

Responsibilities in Marriage

For if the woman be not covered, let her also be shorn: but if it be a shame for a woman to be shorn or shaven, let her be covered. For a man indeed ought not to cover *his* head, forasmuch as he is the image and glory of God: but the woman is the glory of the man. For the man is not of the woman; but the woman of the man. Neither was the man created for the woman; but the woman for the man. For this cause ought the woman to have power on *her* head because of the angels. Nevertheless neither is the man without the woman, neither the woman without the man, in the Lord. For as the woman *is* of the man, even so *is* the man also by the woman; but all things of God. Judge in yourselves: is it comely that a woman pray unto God uncovered? Doth not even nature itself teach you, that, if a man have long hair, it is a shame unto him? But if a woman have long hair, it is a glory to her: for *her* hair is given her for a covering. (1 Corinthians 11:6–15)

Women's liberation is not of God. Yes, we need to be treated fairly, but we are not equal when it comes to the way God created man to be stronger than us and to be our protector. Let us not get this wrong. If you would just look at the disarray in which the world is where fathers and mothers are absent from their children's life, us women need to allow our men to be the priest in our homes. We were designed by our Heavenly Father as the weaker vessel, not to be abused but to be loved and protected.

Likewise, ye wives, *be* in subjection to your own husbands; that, if any obey not the word, they also may without the word be won by the conversation of the wives; While they behold your chaste conversation *coupled* with fear. Whose adorning let it not be that outward *adorning* of plaiting the hair, and of wearing of gold, or of putting on of apparel; But *let it be* the hidden man of the heart, in that which is not corrupt-ible, *even the ornament* of a meek and quiet spirit, which is in the sight of God of great price. For after this manner in the old time the holy women also, who trusted in God, adorned themselves, being in subjection unto their own husbands: Even as Sara obeyed Abraham, calling him lord: whose daughters ye are, as long as ye do well, and are not afraid with any amazement. Likewise, ye husbands, dwell with *them* according to knowl-edge, giving honour unto the wife, as unto the weaker vessel, and as being heirs together of the grace of life; that your prayers be not hindered. (1 Peter 3:1–7)

Husbands, love your wives, even as Christ also loved the church, and gave himself for it; That he might sanctify and cleanse it with the washing of water by the word, That he might present it to himself a glorious church, not hav-ing spot, or wrinkle, or any such thing; but that it should be holy and without blemish. So ought men to love their wives as their own bodies. He that loveth his wife loveth himself. For no man ever yet hated his own flesh; but nourisheth and cherisheth it, even as the Lord the church: For we are members of his body, of his flesh, and of his bones. For this cause shall a man leave his father and mother, and shall be joined unto his wife, and they two shall be one flesh. (Ephesians 5:25–31)

I am writing this book from God's view and not the world's view. Man and woman may make laws to make you comfortable in your sinful lifestyle, but Our Heavenly Father gave us a guideline to live by, and that is his written word no compromise. God's desire is for all men and women to be saved.

> I exhort therefore, that, first of all, supplications, prayers, intercessions, *and* giving of thanks, be made for all men; For kings, and *for* all that are in authority; that we may lead a quiet and peaceable life in all godliness and honesty. For this *is* good and acceptable in the sight of God our Saviour; Who will have all men (when the Bible in this verse uses the word men in this scripture, it is talking about both men, women, boys, and girls) to be saved, and to come unto the knowledge of the truth. For *there* is one God, and one mediator between God and men, the man Christ Jesus; Who gave himself a ransom for all, to be testified in due time. (1 Timothy 2:1–6)

Mary, the Mother of Jesus

We have Mary, the mother Jesus who was impregnated by the Holy Spirit.

> And in the sixth month the angel Gabriel was sent from God unto a city of Galilee, named Nazareth, To a virgin espoused to a man whose name was Joseph, of the house of David; and the virgin's name was Mary. And the angel came in unto her, and said, Hail, *thou that art* highly favoured, the Lord *is* with thee: blessed *art* thou among women. And when she saw *him*, she was troubled at his saying, and cast in her mind what manner of salutation this should be. And the angel said unto her, Fear not, Mary: for thou hast found favour with God. And, behold, thou shalt conceive in thy womb, and bring forth a

son, and shalt call his name JESUS. He shall be great, and shall be called the Son of the Highest: and the Lord God shall give unto him the throne of his father David: And he shall reign over the house of Jacob forever; and of his kingdom there shall be no end. Then said Mary unto the angel, How shall this be, seeing I know not a man? And the angel answered and said unto her, The Holy Ghost shall come upon thee, and the power of the Highest shall overshadow thee: therefore also that holy thing which shall be born of thee shall be called the Son of God. (Luke 1:26–35)

Elisabeth, Wife of Zacharias and Mother of John the Baptist, Foreteller of Jesus Christ

And, behold, thy cousin Elisabeth, she hath also conceived a son in her old age: and this is the sixth month with her, who was called barren. For with God nothing shall be impossible. And Mary said, Behold the handmaid of the Lord; be it unto me according to thy word. And the angel departed from her. And Mary arose in those days, and went into the hill country with haste, into a city of Juda; And entered into the house of Zacharias, and saluted Elisabeth. And it came to pass, that, when Elisabeth heard the salutation of Mary, the babe leaped in her womb; and Elisabeth was filled with the Holy Ghost: And she spake out with a loud voice, and said, Blessed *art* thou among women, and blessed *is* the fruit of thy womb. And whence *is* this to me, that the mother of my Lord should come to me? For, lo, as soon as the voice of thy salutation sounded in mine ears, the babe leaped in my womb for joy. (Luke 1:36–44)

Gomer, Wife of Hosea the Prophet

Gomer is the wife of Hosea, the prophet who God commanded him to marry. Gomer was a whore who symbolized the great whoredom by the children of Israel the land had committed. The children's name they had together symbolized the different things that would happen. Please read Hosea 1:2–9:

> The beginning of the word of the Lord by Hosea. And the Lord said to Hosea, Go, take unto thee a wife of whoredoms and children of whoredoms: for the land hath committed great whoredom, *departing* from the Lord. So he went and took Gomer the daughter of Diblaim; which conceived, and bare him a son. And the Lord said unto him, Call his name Jezreel; for yet a little *while*, and I will avenge the blood of Jezreel upon the house of Jehu, and will cause to cease the kingdom of the house of Israel. And it shall come to pass at that day, that I will break the bow of Israel, in the valley of Jezreel. And she conceived again, and bare a daughter. And *God* said unto him, Call her name Loruhamah: for I will no more have mercy upon the house of Israel; but I will utterly take them away. But I will have mercy upon the house of Judah, and will save them by the Lord their God, and will not save them by bow, nor by sword, nor by battle, by horses, nor by horsemen. Now when she had weaned Loruhamah, she conceived, and bare a son. Then said *God*, Call his name Loammi: for ye *are* not my people, and I will not be your *God*.

Mary Magdalene

So my list goes on with female presence in the Bible. *Mary Magdalene is next.* I will write of Mary Magdalene. I will call her

Mary M. Those of you that already know Mary M's story may ask why I chose Mary M. Well, I am going to say it like God's word says it.

> For my thoughts *are* not your thoughts, neither *are* your ways my ways, saith the Lord. For as the heavens are higher than the earth, so are my ways higher than your ways, and my thoughts than your thoughts. For as the rain cometh down, and the snow from heaven, and returneth not thither, but watereth the earth, and maketh it bring forth and bud, that it may give seed to the sower, and bread to the eater: So shall my word be that goeth forth out of my mouth: it shall not return unto me void, but it shall accomplish that which I please, and it shall prosper *in the thing* whereto I sent it. (Isaiah 55:8–11)

> Because the foolishness of God is wiser than men; and the weakness of God is stronger than men. For ye see your calling, brethren, how that not many wise men after the flesh, not many mighty, not many noble, *are called*: But God hath chosen the foolish things of the world to confound the wise; and God hath chosen the weak things of the world to confound the things which are mighty; And base things of the world, and things which are despised, hath God chosen, *yea*, and things which are not, to bring to nought things that are: That no flesh should glory in his presence. (1 Corinthians 1:25–29)

Mary M. was delivered of seven demons.

"And a certain women, which had been healed of evil spirits and infirmities. Mary called Magdalene, out of whom went seven devils.

And Joanna the wife of Chuza Herod's steward, and Susanna, and many others, which ministered unto him of their substance" (Luke 8:2).

> And, behold, a woman in the city, which was a sinner, when she knew that *Jesus* sat at meat in the Pharisee's house, brought an alabaster box of ointment, And stood at his feet behind *him* weeping, and began to wash his feet with tears, and did wipe *them* with the hairs of her head, and kissed his feet, and anointed *them* with the ointment. Now when the Pharisee which had bidden him saw *it*, he spake within himself, saying, This man, if he were a prophet, would have known who and what manner of woman *this is* that toucheth him: for she is a sinner. (Luke 7:37–39)

> And it came to pass, when Jesus had finished all these sayings, he said unto his disciples, Ye know that after two days is *the feast of* the passover, and the Son of man is betrayed to be crucified. Then assembled together the chief priests, and the scribes, and the elders of the people, unto the palace of the high priest, who was called Caiaphas, And consulted that they might take Jesus by subtilty, and kill *him*. But they said, Not on the feast *day*, lest there be an uproar among the people. Now when Jesus was in Bethany, in the house of Simon the leper, There came unto him a woman having an alabaster box of very precious ointment, and poured it on his head, as he sat *at m*eat. But when his disciples saw *it*, they had indignation, saying, To what purpose is this waste? For this ointment might have been sold for much, and given to the poor. When Jesus understood *it*, he said unto them, Why trouble

ye the woman? for she hath wrought a good work upon me. For ye have the poor always with you; but me ye have not always. For in that she hath poured this ointment on my body, she did it for my burial. Verily I say unto you, Wheresoever this gospel shall be preached in the whole world, *there* shall also this, that this woman hath done, be told for a memorial of her. (Matthew 26:1–13)

I submit to you that this woman is Mary M. Jesus said in Matthew 26:13, "Verily I say unto you, Wheresoever this gospel shall be preached in the whole world, there shall also this, that this woman hath done, be told for a memorial of her." Mary M. is a woman and a disciple of Jesus, and she is remembered in all four gospels and present at his crucifixion, death, burial, and resurrection. I believe the scripture in Matthew 26:13 is why the Holy Spirit is having me write of Mary M. as I call her, no disrespect at all.

And about the ninth hour Jesus cried with a loud voice, saying, Eli, Eli, lama sabachthani? that is to say, My God, my God, why hast thou forsaken me? Some of them that stood there, when they heard *that*, said, This *man* calleth for Elias. And straightway one of them ran, and took a spunge, and filled *it* with vinegar, and put *it* on a reed, and gave him to drink. The rest said, Let be, let us see whether Elias will come to save him. Jesus, when he had cried again with a loud voice, yielded up the ghost. (Matthew 27:46–50)

And many women were there beholding afar off, which followed Jesus from Galilee, ministering unto him:
Among which was Mary Magdalene, and Mary the mother of James and Joses, and the mother of Zebedee's children. When the even

was come, there came a rich man of Arimathaea, named Joseph, who also himself was Jesus' disciple: He went to Pilate, and begged the body of Jesus. Then Pilate commanded the body to be delivered. And when Joseph had taken the body, he wrapped it in a clean linen cloth, And laid it in his own new tomb, which he had hewn out in the rock: and he rolled a great stone to the door of the sepulchre, and departed. And there was Mary Magdalene, and the other Mary, sitting over against the sepulchre. Now the next day, that followed the day of the preparation, the chief priests and Pharisees came together unto Pilate, Saying, Sir, we remember that that deceiver said, while he was yet alive, After three days I will rise again. Command therefore that the sepulchre be made sure until the third day, lest his disciples come by night, and steal him away, and say unto the people, He is risen from the dead: so the last error shall be worse than the first. Pilate said unto them, Ye have a watch: go your way, make *it* as sure as ye can. So they went, and made the sepulchre sure, sealing the stone, and setting a watch. (Matthew 27:55–66)

In the end of the sabbath, as it began to dawn toward the first *day* of the week, came Mary Magdalene and the other Mary to see the sepulchre. And, behold, there was a great earthquake: for the angel of the Lord descended from heaven, and came and rolled back the stone from the door, and sat upon it. His countenance was like lightning, and his raiment white as snow: And for fear of him the keepers did shake, and became as dead *men*. And the angel answered and said unto the women, Fear not ye: for I know that ye seek

Jesus, which was crucified. He is not here: for he is risen, as he said. Come, see the place where the Lord lay. And go quickly, and tell his disciples that he is risen from the dead; and, behold, he goeth before you into Galilee; there shall ye see him: lo, I have told you. And they departed quickly from the sepulchre with fear and great joy; and did run to bring his disciples word. And as they went to tell his disciples, behold, Jesus met them, saying, All hail. And they came and held him by the feet, and worshipped him. Then said Jesus unto them, Be not afraid: go tell my brethren that they go into Galilee, and there shall they see me. (Matthew 28:1–10)

Not only did the angel in Matthew 28:2 place Mary M. into ministry after Jesus' resurrection by telling her to go tell the other disciples that Jesus has risen and is alive, but Jesus himself in Matthew 28:10, "Then said Jesus unto them, be not afraid: go tell, my brethren that they go into Galilee, and there shall they see me." Jesus put Mary M. along with the other women that were with her into ministry. Mary M. is present Jesus crucifixion, death, burial and resurrection.

Deborah

Deborah was a prophetess, the wife of Lapidoth. She judged Israel at the time. Deborah had to encourage Barak to follow through with God's instruction to draw toward Tabor and take ten thousand men. Barak would not go unless Deborah went with him. Read about it in Judges 4:4–10.

Esther

Esther became a queen and replaced Queen Vashti, and she risked herself to save her people. Read about it in the book named after her.

Hannah

The mother of Samuel. She asked for a child and promised to hand him to the Lord.

Sarai

Sarai became *Sarah*. She had a child in her old age. She was the wife of Abraham, the father of many nations.

<u>Women in Ministry with Jesus</u>

There were always women in the ministry in Jesus' time all the way up until his death, burial, and resurrection. "And many women were there beholding afar off, which followed Jesus from Galilee, ministering unto him: Among which was Mary Magdalene, and Mary the mother of James and Joses, and the mother of Zebedee's children" (Matthew 27:55–56).

Meanwhile, read the Word of God for yourself; do not let the world, man, or woman tell you that you are not valuable to God and that women are not to speak or teach in the church. I encourage you to mediate on God's word day and night.

> This book of the law shall not depart out of thy mouth; but thou shalt meditate therein day and night, that thou mayest observe to do according to all that is written therein: for then thou shalt make thy way prosperous, and then thou shalt have good success. (Joshua 1:8)

> Blessed *is* the man that walketh not in the counsel of the ungodly, nor standeth in the way of sinners, nor sinneth in the seat of the scornful. But his delight *is* in the law of the LORD; and in his law doth he meditate day and night. And he shall be like a tree planted by the rivers of water,

that bringeth forth his fruit in his season; his leaf also shall not wither; and whatsoever he doeth shall prosper. (Psalm 1:1–3)

11

Are You Putting on Your Armor Daily?

Put on the whole Armor of God, that ye may be
able to stand against the wiles of the devil.

—Ephesians 6:11

For the years that I have been in church, I have been hearing about putting on the armor of God. Until recently, I really was not sure what it meant. I believe it was because the years that I had been in church, the law had been preached over my head when Jesus fulfilled the law. By the law being taught and preached to me, it just caused me to stay in sin. I still struggled up until two years ago. Then I read a book about putting on the armor of God. I now understand about putting on the armor of God daily. I went through a deliverance from being demonize.

> When the unclean spirit is gone out of a man, he walketh through dry places, seeking rest, and findeth none. Then he saith, I will return into my house from whence I came out; and when he is come, he findeth *it* empty, swept, and garnished. Then goeth he, and taketh with himself seven other spirits more wicked than himself, and they enter in and dwell there: and the

last *state* of that man is worse than the first. Even
so shall it be also unto this wicked generation.
(Matthew 12:43–45)

Believe that when we keep struggling in sin day in and day out,
there is something wrong. This is not normal. You may need to be
delivered of being demonized. I now understand that I personally
cannot do the same things or hang with ungodly family and friends.
James 4:4 says, "Ye adulterers and adulteresses, know ye not that the
friendship of the world is enmity with God? whosoever therefore
will be a friend of the world is the enemy of God." For those of you
who may be saying I never slept with someone's husband, permit
me to give you the Bible's definition of what this scripture says: An
adulterer is one who is faithless toward God, and those who relapse
into idolatry are said to commit adultery or play the harlot and are
faithless to God, unclean, apostate. So whatever your idol is, whether
it be that shiny new car, those fingers or hand that masturbate, day or
nighttime soaps, gossip or listening to gossip, or gossip about celeb-
rity, watching ungodly television or internet movies, or music that
glorifies the flesh and ungodly living, etc., these all are enemy of God.

I have been guilty of it all. I just recently let go of my music that
I loved listening to when I traveled. I recently got a revelation that I
had to let it go. Even if you can find a godly movie or show on television, the commercials are so filled with death and negatively spoken
words. And Romans 8:7–21 says,

Because the carnal mind *is* enmity against
God: for it is not subject to the law of God, nei-
ther indeed can be. So then they that are in the
flesh cannot please God. But ye are not in the
flesh, but in the Spirit, if so be that the Spirit of
God dwell in you. Now if any man have not the
Spirit of Christ, he is none of his. And if Christ
be in you, the body *is* dead because of sin; but the
Spirit *is* life because of righteousness. But if the
Spirit of him that raised up Jesus from the dead

dwell in you, he that raised up Christ from the dead shall also quicken your mortal bodies by his Spirit that dwelleth in you. Therefore, brethren, we are debtors, not to the flesh, to live after the flesh. For if ye live after the flesh, ye shall die: but if ye through the Spirit do mortify the deeds of the body, ye shall live. For as many as are led by the Spirit of God, they are the sons of God. For ye have not received the spirit of bondage again to fear; but ye have received the Spirit of adoption, whereby we cry, Abba, Father. The Spirit itself beareth witness with our spirit, that we are the children of God: And if children, then heirs; heirs of God, and joint-heirs with Christ; if so be that we suffer with *him*, that we may be also glorified together. For I reckon that the sufferings of this present time *are* not worthy *to be compared* with the glory which shall be revealed in us. For the earnest expectation of the creature waiteth for the manifestation of the sons of God. For the creature was made subject to vanity, not willingly, but by reason of him who hath subjected *the same* in hope, Because the creature itself also shall be delivered from the bondage of corruption into the glorious liberty of the children of God.

There is, therefore, now no condemnation to them which are in Christ Jesus, who walk not after the flesh but after the Spirit. I think we have forgotten about the last part of that scripture, "who walk not after the flesh." I personally had not been walking in the Spirit but after my flesh. I have been pleasing my flesh. I used to always read the first part of that scripture: "There is no condemnation to those who are in Christ Jesus." I have repented and have been delivered. I am staying in the word and putting on the armor of God daily and staying in God's word. I am learning to make it a priority over anything else in my life. You may say it does not take all of this. I probably even said that myself. It takes all of that for me. If people would be honest with themselves, it does take every bit of putting on the armor of God daily. Once you get delivered of ungodly soul ties, unforgiveness, negative spoken words, or doctors' diagnoses, and generational curses, you do not want these things to come back on you.

> When the unclean spirit is gone out of a man, he walketh through dry places, seeking rest, and findeth none. Then he saith, I will return into my house from whence I came out; and when he is come, he findeth *it* empty, swept, and garnished. Then goeth he, and taketh with himself seven other spirits more wicked than himself, and they enter in and dwell there: and the last *state* of that man is worse than the first. Even so shall it be also unto this wicked generation. (Matthew 12:43–45)

After you have been delivered of ungodly soul ties, unforgiveness, negative, spoken words, or doctors' diagnoses, and generational curses, you want to keep your deliverance because Satan will try to return. He only leaves for a season. "And when the devil had ended all the temptation, he departed from him (Jesus) for a season" (Luke 4:13). Now if the devil continued to pursue Jesus, who do we think we are that he won't come back after us? You must continue to stay in the full armor of God daily. It is important to stay balanced. Eat healthy meals, get rest and sleep and some form of exercise; if you just do some form of exercise daily, do consult your doctor first. The devil likes to come in when we are hungry, angry, lonely, or tired (HALT). It is okay to be angry if you do not allow it to turn to sin. "Be ye angry, and sin not: let not the sun go down upon your wrath: Neither give place to the devil" (Ephesians 4:26–27).

Now, I am finally out of the wilderness. I want to stay out of the wilderness. How do I plan to do this? I will daily put on the whole armor of God (Ephesian 6:10–18), and I keep my mind stayed on God. "Thou wilt keep *him* in perfect peace, *whose* mind *is* stayed on *thee*; because he trusteth in thee" (Isaiah 26:3). You must be vigilant to watch over yourself because the devil seeks who he may devour. "Be sober, be vigilant; because your adversary the devil, as a roaring lion, walketh about, seeking whom he may devour" (1 Peter 5:8). "The thief cometh not, but for to steal, and to kill, and to destroy: I am come that they might have life, and they might have *it* more abundantly" (John 10:10).

This scripture is written in red, which means Jesus is speaking. I am pleading with you to choose life. Jesus gives life. "I call heaven and earth to record this day against you, *that* I have set before you life and death, blessing and cursing: therefore choose life, that both thou and thy seed may live" (Deuteronomy 30:19–20). God gives you a test and gives you the answer right in the scriptures. If only we would read and meditate on God's word.

> That thou mayest love the LORD thy God, *and* that thou mayest obey his voice, and that thou mayest cleave unto him: for he *is* thy life, and the length of thy days: that thou mayest dwell in the land which the LORD sware unto thy fathers, to Abraham, to Isaac, and to Jacob, to give them. (Deuteronomy 30:20)

We are Abraham's seed. Choose life with the words of your mouth. "Death and life *are* in the power of the tongue: and they that love it shall eat the fruit thereof" (Proverbs 18:21). God's word, the Bible, is a book of instruction for godly living.

> And that from a child thou hast known the holy scriptures, which are able to make thee wise unto salvation through faith which is in Christ Jesus. All scripture *is* given by inspiration of God, and *is* profitable for doctrine for reproof, for correction, for instruction in righteousness: That the man of God may be perfect, thoroughly furnished unto all good works. (2 Timothy 3:15–17)

> And if ye *be* Christ's, then are ye Abraham's
> seed, and heirs according to the promise.
> (Galatians 3:29)

I am no longer at the well. I have now left the well and choose to sit at Jesus feet by listening to the word every chance that I get an opportunity to hear. Jesus is living on the inside of me through the in dwelling of the Holy Spirit. I may not be able to sit at Jesus' feet the way Mary of Bethany did, but I have Jesus living on the inside of me through the Holy Spirit.

12

The Struggle and the Struggle Being Over

> Keeping mercy for thousands, forgiving iniquity
> and transgression and sin, and that will by no means
> clear *the guilty*; visiting the iniquity of the fathers
> upon the children, and upon the children's children,
> unto the third and to the fourth *generation*.
>
> —Exodus 34:7

I was sitting up watching one of my YouTube shows I subscribe to when I heard the author of her new book say, "Be honest and open." So this morning, in the bathroom, as I was removing facial hairs, I was thinking about what this new author had said last night. As I was meditating on what she said, the Holy Spirit gave me another two or three chapters to write. When my Heavenly Father told me it was time to finish the book, I was still living with the man. I was shacked up in his house but no longer in his bed.

Early on, I told this man that I do not know how long I could do this because I know me living with him and having sex with him is wrong. It was about two months into this living arrangement that I told this man I could no longer have sex with him, and I eventually moved into the other bedroom. During this two months, I was told I had to move quite a few times. I had made up in my mind that I was going to move when I finished Bible college. Imagine that; I was in Bible college. I believe this is why I told this man when I did that I could not no longer have sex with him. I knew the school had a standard, and I did not want to come to school on a lie.

Wow, forget the schools standard. What about God's written word to me and his standard? That should have been enough for me not to move into the situation in the first place. So things got volatile to the point of domestic violence. I was still cleaning this man's house and cooking a few meals here and there. I finally got tired of this man being controlling, and I spoke up about it one day. This was when this man yelled out, "I will be glad when you move." So I knew what he said in anger was how he really felt.

> O generation of viper, how can ye, being evil, speak good things? For out of the abundance of the heart the mouth speaketh. A good man out of the good treasure of the heart bringeth forth good things: and an evil man out of the evil treasure bringeth forth evil things. (Matthew 12:34–35)

I still had love in my heart for this man because when Sheila loves, she loves hard. You know, if I truly loved him, I would have never put him in this position. I knew the word well enough that I had no business giving into his offer to rent a room that turned into shacking. It would have been a better witness if I had said no to this situation. To be completely honest, I believed I used this man to get back to Minnesota to finish out my school program at the Bible college. A school that used the Bible for its textbook. I did not know how to protect my boundaries, and I realized later I needed deliverance to break some soul ties, renounce some things in my family lineage such as the Free Masons, and break generational curses.

When God told me that it was time to finish this book in early 2020, I was still struggling, still worrying about giving into fornication. I was still fornicating all the way up until January 2021. I reached out for help. I joined a support group where I would hear other women be honest about where they were struggling, and I would learn some things. It was on June 25, 2021, that I had my first deliverance done on me. You know that some churches and men of God teach that if you don't believe such things as being demonized or being demon-possessed, it can't happen to you; or there is no such thing as generational curse, when God's Word clearly talks about generational curses.

"Jesus Christ is the same yesterday, today and forever" (Hebrews 13:8). Well, before my deliverance, the demonic spirit of incubus or succubus came on me so strong, it was as though something invisible was stimulating my private area. This sensation was so strong on me. This demonic spirit was on me so strong that. I gave into the urges. I gave in to pleasure myself. I knew for sure after this event that I needed deliverance. I would like to do a forty-day fast just to spend that time with my Heavenly Father.

> And when they were come to the multitude, there came to him a *certain* man, kneeling down to him, and saying, Lord, have mercy on my son: for he is lunatick, and sore vexed: for ofttimes he falleth into the fire, and oft into the water. And I brought him to thy disciples, and they could not cure him. Then Jesus answered and said, O faithless and perverse generation, how long shall I be with you? How long shall I suffer you? Bring him hither to me. And Jesus rebuked the devil; and he departed out of him: and the child was cured from that very hour. Then came the disciples to Jesus apart, and said, Why could not we cast him out? And Jesus said unto them, Because of your unbelief: for verily I say unto you, If ye have faith as a grain of mustard seed, ye shall say unto this mountain, Remove hence to yonder place; and it shall remove; and nothing shall be impossible unto you. Howbeit this kind goeth not out but by prayer and fasting. (Matthew 17:14–21)

Some things are so strong down your family lineage that it will take a fast to break some things off of you. If you are going to make a change, you must get serious about what God says in his Word. If you don't take some serious steps such as deliverance and a serious fast, these curses will continue down your family line. Do remember Proverbs 26:2: "As a bird by wandering, as the swallow by flying, so the curse causeless shall not come."

13

My People Are Destroyed for Ignorance of God's Law

My people are destroyed for lack of knowledge: because thou hast rejected knowledge, I will also reject thee, that thou shalt be no priest to me: seeing thou hast forgotten the law of thy God, I will also forget thy children.

—Hosea 4:6

Years ago, after joining what I will call my first real church where I began to learn of God's Word, through this church, God began to heal me of some things, such as codependence and being a little less dysfunctional. My Heavenly Father began the work. I remembered praying this prayer in 1984: "God, don't ever allow me to think that I have arrived. Always let me be a growing, maturing Christian."

It is 2003, and God's has honored the sincerity of my prayer all these years ago. I believe that the enemy, the devil, Satan, whatever you want to call him, yes, he is real; and he is using some churches to keep his people ignorant. The word says, "Study to shew thyself approved unto God, a workman that needeth not to be ashamed, rightly dividing the word of truth" (2 Timothy 2:15). It is our responsibility to search and study the scriptures for ourselves. How do you allow a man or a person to tell us such things as there is no Holy Spirit and speaking in tongues went out with the old church?

> Follow after charity, and desire spiritual *gifts*, but rather that ye may prophesy. For he that speaketh in an *unknown* tongue speaketh not unto men, but unto God: for no man understandeth *him*; howbeit in the spirit he speaketh mysteries. But he that prophesieth speaketh unto men *to* edification, and exhortation, and comfort. He that speaketh in an *unknown* tongue edifieth himself; but he that prophesieth edifieth the church. (1 Corinthians 14:1–4)

I believe that people have been taught wrong about this scripture I am about to share with you. First Corinthians chapter 12 talks about spiritual gifts.

> *Now concerning spiritual gifts, brethren, I would not have you ignorant. Ye know that ye were Gentiles, carried away unto these dumb idols, even as ye were led. Wherefore I give you to understand, that no man speaking by the Spirit of God calleth Jesus accursed: and that no man can say that Jesus is the Lord, but by the Holy Ghost. Now there are diversities of gifts, but the same Spirit. And there are differences of administrations, but the same Lord. And there are diversities of operations, but it is the same God which worketh all in all. But the manifestation of the Spirit is given to every man to profit withal. For to one is given by the Spirit the word of wisdom; to another the word of knowledge by the same Spirit; To another faith by the same Spirit; to another the gifts of healing by the same Spirit; To another the working of miracles; to another prophecy; to another discerning of spirits; to another divers kinds of tongues; to another*

the interpretation of tongues: <u>*But all these worketh that one and the selfsame Spirit, dividing to every man severally as he will.*</u> For as the body is one, and hath many members, and all the members of that one body, being many, are one body: so also *is* Christ. For by one Spirit are we all baptized into one body, whether we be Jews or Gentiles, whether *we be* bond or free; and have been all made to drink into one Spirit.

For the body is not one member, but many. If the foot shall say, Because I am not the hand, I am not of the body; is it therefore not of the body? And if the ear shall say, Because I am not the eye, I am not of the body; is it therefore not of the body? If the whole body *were* an eye, where *were* the hearing? If the whole *were* hearing, where *were* the smelling? But now hath God set the members every one of them in the body, as it hath pleased him. And if they were all one member, where *were* the body? But now *are they* many members, yet but one body. And the eye cannot say unto the hand, I have no need of thee: nor again the head to the feet, I have no need of you. Nay, much more those members of the body, which seem to be more feeble, are necessary: And those *members* of the body, which we think to be less honourable, upon these we bestow more abundant honour; and our uncomely *parts* have more abundant comeliness. For our comely *parts* have no need: but God hath tempered the body together, having given more abundant honour to that *part* which lacked. That there should be no schism in the body; but *that* the members should have the same care one for another. And whether one member suffer, all the members suffer with it; or one member be honoured, all the members rejoice with it. Now ye are the body of Christ, and members in particular. *And God hath set some in the church, first apostles, secondarily prophets, thirdly teachers, after that miracles, then gifts of healings, helps, governments, diversities of tongues. Are all apostles? are all prophets? are all teachers? are all workers of miracles? Have all the gifts of healing? do all speak with tongues? do all interpret? But covet earnestly the best gifts: and yet shew I unto you a more excellent way.* (1 Corinthians 12:1–31)

Now, I have put in italics the scriptures. I believe the scripture in 1 Corinthians 12:11 is why some people think you should not be able to pray in your prayer language as you will because this is taught wrong in some churches. But you have to search it out for yourself. The Bible says in 1 John 2:27, "But the anointing which ye have received of him abideth in you, and ye need not that any man teach you: but as the same anointing teacheth you of all things, and is truth and no lie, and even as it hath taught you, ye shall abide in him." I hear people say at funerals also, "The Lord giveth and the Lord taketh way." They are taking scriptures out of context. "And said, Naked came I out of my mother's womb, and naked shall I return thither: the LORD gave, and the LORD hath taken away; blessed be the name of the LORD" (Job 1:21). That is like saying it is okay to have sex with another's man wife the way that King David did with Bathsheba, another man's wife, because it is in the Bible.

Not only did he do that; Bathsheba got pregnant when King David could not get Uriah to go home and have sex with his wife because Uriah would not enjoy the comforts of home when the other men were on the battlefield due to his loyalty. So King David set him up to be murdered on the front line. God, our Heavenly Father, does not take people away without there being a cause. Our God is a good Father. You must read the Bible in context. People in the church are just repeating what they heard another man in the pulpit say. I will be surprised if they have even read the whole book of Job.

"Jesus Christ is the same yesterday and today and forever" (Hebrews 13:8). Or they would say things like there is no such thing as generational curses. That is exactly what the devil and his foes want you to believe. I believe that because of my prayer, all those years ago of to always be a growing, maturing Christian. God has always gotten information to me to help me grow.

God is able to break the generational curses in your lives, but you need to be aware of them. If you are having premature deaths, murder, cancer, etc., in your family, those are generational curses that need to be broken. You first need to give your life to God and accept Jesus Christ as your Lord and Savior.

> And when they were come to the multitude, there came to him a *certain* man, kneeling down to him, and saying, Lord, have mercy on my son: for he is lunatick, and sore vexed: for ofttimes he falleth into the fire, and oft into the water. And I brought him to thy disciples, and they could not cure him. Then Jesus answered and said, O faithless and perverse generation, how long shall I be with you? how long shall I suffer you? bring him hither to me. And Jesus rebuked the devil; and he departed out of him: and the child was cured from that very hour. Then came the disciples to Jesus apart, and said, Why could not we cast him out? And Jesus said unto them, Because of your unbelief: for verily I say unto you, If ye have faith as a grain of mustard seed, ye shall say unto this mountain, Remove hence to yonder place; and it shall remove; and nothing shall be impossible unto you. Howbeit this kind goeth not out but by prayer and fasting. (Matthew 17:14–21)

Do not stay ignorant of the truth once you get saved. The Holy Spirit is your comforter and teacher.

> If ye shall ask any thing in my name, I will do *it*. If ye love me, keep my commandments.

And I will pray the Father, and he shall give you another Comforter, that he may abide with you for ever; *Even* the Spirit of truth; whom the world cannot receive, because it seeth him not, neither knoweth him: but ye know him; for he dwelleth with you, and shall be in you. I will not leave you comfortless: I will come to you. Yet a little while, and the world seeth me no more; but ye see me: because I live, ye shall live also. At that day ye shall know that I *am* in my Father, and ye in me, and I in you. He that hath my commandments, and keepeth them, he it is that loveth me: and he that loveth me shall be loved of my Father, and I will love him, and will manifest myself to him. Judas saith unto him, not Iscariot, Lord, how is it that thou wilt manifest thyself unto us, and not unto the world? Jesus answered and said unto him, If a man love me, he will keep my words: and my Father will love him, and we will come unto him, and make our abode with him. He that loveth me not keepeth not my sayings: and the word which ye hear is not mine, but the Father's which sent me. These things have I spoken unto you, being *yet* present with you. But the Comforter, *which is* the Holy Ghost, whom the Father will send in my name, he shall teach you all things, and bring all things to your remembrance, whatsoever I have said unto you. (John 14:14–26)

So I plead; I beg you to study the Word of God for yourself and rely on the Holy Spirit to give you revelation knowledge. "But the anointing which ye have received of him abideth in you, and ye need not that any man teach you: but as the same anointing teacheth you of all things, and is truth, and is no lie, and even as it hath taught you, ye shall abide in him" (1 John 2:27). Take God's Word and read and meditate on it until you get the truth.

14

After Deliverance: One Year-Plus Later

And ye shall know the truth, and the
truth shall make you free.

—John 8:32

I had completed my book on December 1, 2021, but now I felt led to see if the Holy Spirit had any other chapters for me to write before I had the book published. So I printed out the last manuscript. While my pages were printing out, I prayed to the Holy Spirit to see if he had any other chapters for me to write, and I decreed that I should be able to just look at my table of contents and sense if there was another chapter for me to write. This is what I heard: "After Deliverance and sequel." So God may want me to write a sequel to this book. This is what I heard in my spirit. I said for now, I would just write what the Holy Spirit gives me for this chapter. I had written out another whole chapter and thought I had saved it, but somehow, it was not where I thought I had saved it. Thankfully, I had printed out the beginning of what I had written, so that saved me a little time.

So here goes: One year ago, on June 25, 2021, I had prepared to go through my first deliverance for myself. I read Gina S. Valdez's book, *Put on the Whole Armor of God, Deliverance Edition*. I did my preparation to prepare for deliverance assigned to me through her ministry. On June 25, 2022, it was my anniversary date, and believe me, I celebrated. I went through two more deliverances before I began to feel something different. I felt freedom that I never felt before.

I lived in fear for years that I was going to disappoint God and fall into sexual immorality, and I did. This time was different. I did not feel any fear. After my deliverance, I no longer lived in fear. The Bible school I attended said we gave Satan too much credit; instead of paying so much attention to Satan and his demons, we should be talking about what Jesus could do. At least that is the way that I interpreted what I heard. Well, that may work for others, but I needed something more after I left Bible school. Maybe my fellow classmates had the knowledge they needed to get delivered before attending Bible school or during Bible school to get delivered. "Through knowledge shall the just be delivered" (Proverbs 11:9b).

I had been a victim of gang rape, rape, physical abuse, rejections in the womb, and only God knows what else. You know they, evil spirits, have the legal right to come back, but you do not have to give in to them, but they have the legal right to try.

> When the unclean spirit is gone out of a man, he walketh through dry places, seeking rest, and findeth none. Then he saith, I will return into my house from whence I came out; and when he is come, he findeth it empty, swept, and garnished. Then goeth he, and taketh with himself seven other spirits more wicked than himself, and they enter in and dwell there: and the last *state* of that man is worse than the first. Even so shall it be also unto this wicked generation. (Matthew 12:43–45)

When the Holy Spirit showed me in 1989, at my kitchen window after asking the question why I felt a need to spend time with another man other than the man I was in a relationship with, married or not, this lengthy conversation between me and the Holy Spirit ensued. What came out of that conversation with the Holy Spirit and myself was he told me I was rejected in my mother's womb. I called my mother the next day, and she told me she was going to give me up for adoption if I was a girl. One of my aunts talked her out of giving me away. We had a wonderful conversation that day.

So once I could put my hand on the problem, I prayed through, and I have not had that issue anymore. I made sure in my deliverance time to include rejection, just to be sure. The people of God talked about deliverance throughout the New Testament. Curses still do occur. People are practicing witchcraft all the time, and we had better learn what to do to get it off us and keep it off us. Proverbs 26:2 says, "As the bird by wandering, as the swallow by flying, so the curse causeless shall not come." We had better get off excessively being on social media and learn what God's word says, me included.

There is so much freedom and peace after deliverance. There are good books out there on deliverance. I would suggest you keep your Bible nearby to make sure it is scripturally sound. Here I am in my sixties when I finally received deliverance from things. I could have been free years ago. They say God's timing is perfect. I was forty years old when my Heavenly Father gave me this book to write. I was sixty-two when my Heavenly Father told me it was time to finish the book. So I finished the book, but the Holy Spirit gave me this last chapter.

I am sensing there may be another book to this one. When I first begin truly learning about the things of God in my twenties, I asked my Heavenly Father to never let me think that I have arrived and allow me to always be a growing maturing Christian. My Heavenly Father honored and continues to honor that prayer. It reminds of the prayer Solomon said in a dream.

> And Solomon loved the LORD, walking in the statutes of David his father: only he sacrificed and burnt incense in high places. And the king went to Gibeon to sacrifice there; for that *was* the great high place: a thousand burnt offerings did Solomon offer upon that altar. In Gibeon the LORD appeared to Solomon in a dream by night:

and God said, Ask what I shall give thee. And Solomon said, Thou hast shewed unto thy servant David my father great mercy, according as he walked before thee in truth, and in righteousness, and in uprightness of heart with thee; and thou hast kept for him this great kindness, that thou hast given him a son to sit on his throne, as *it is* this day. And now, O Lord my God, thou hast made thy servant king instead of David my father: and I *am but* a little child: I know not *how* to go out or come in. And thy servant *is* in the midst of thy people which thou hast chosen, a great people, that cannot be numbered nor counted for multitude. Give therefore thy servant an understanding heart to judge thy people, that I may discern between good and bad: for who is able to judge this thy so great a people? And the speech pleased the Lord, that Solomon had asked this thing. And God said unto him, Because thou hast asked this thing, and hast not asked for thyself long life; neither hast asked riches for thyself, nor hast asked the life of thine enemies; but hast asked for thyself understanding to discern judgment; Behold, I have done according to thy words: lo, I have given thee a wise and an understanding heart; so that there was none like thee before thee, neither after thee shall any arise like unto thee. And I have also given thee that which thou hast not asked, both riches, and honour: so that there shall not be any among the kings like unto thee all thy days. And if thou wilt walk in my ways, to keep my statutes and my commandments, as thy father David did walk, then I will lengthen thy days. And Solomon awoke; and, behold, *it was* a dream. And he came to Jerusalem, and stood before the ark of the covenant of the Lord, and offered up burnt offerings, and offered peace offerings, and made a feast to all his servants. (1 Kings 3:3–15)

A short time later, King Solomon had a situation to judge:

> Then came there two women, *that were* harlots, unto the king, and stood before him. And the one woman said, O my lord, I and this woman dwell in one house; and I was delivered of a child with her in the house. And it came to pass the third day after that I was delivered, that this woman was delivered also: and we were together; *there was* no stranger with us in the house, save we two in the house. And this woman's child died in the night; because she overlaid it. And she arose at midnight, and took my son from beside me, while thine handmaid slept, and laid it in her bosom, and laid her dead child in my bosom. And when I rose in the morning to give my child suck, behold, it was dead: but when I had considered it in the morning, behold, it was not my son, which I did bear. And the other woman said, Nay; but the living *is* my son, and the dead *is* thy son. And this said, No; but the dead is thy son, and the living *is* my son. Thus they spake before the king. Then said the king, The one saith, This *is* my son that liveth, and thy son *is* the dead: and the other saith, Nay; but thy son *is* the dead, and my son *is* the living. And the king said, Bring me a sword. And they brought a sword before the king. And the king said, Divide the living child in two, and give half to the one, and half to the other. Then spake the woman whose the living child *was* unto the king, for her bowels yearned upon her son, and she said, O my lord, give her the living child, and in no wise slay it. But the other said, Let it

be neither mine nor thine, *but* divide *it*. Then the king answered and said, Give her the living child, and in no wise slay it: she *is* the mother thereof. And all Israel heard of the judgment which the king had judged; and they feared the king: for they saw that the wisdom of God *was* in him, to do judgment. (1 Kings 3:16–28)

We can see that God answered King Solomon's prayer from his dream. I may have left churches without seeking my Heavenly Father about it, or I may be moved to other locations because of a relationship, but through it all, God has continued to take me deeper in the things of God. My Heavenly Father has allowed me through people that I am acquainted with to find great teachers on the internet that has opened my eyes to things I did not learn in my church. It might have been taught, but I did not learn it. The thing that I have learned away from churches was all based on the Word of God. People need deliverance, and they or not taught about deliverance in a lot of churches. They are taught to sow a seed for this or that to get healed or to get blessed. God's Word said, "By Jesus' stripes you were healed" (1 Peter 2:24). God's Word also said in Ephesians 1:3, "Blessed *be* the God and Father of our Lord Jesus Christ, who hath blessed us with all spiritual blessings in heavenly *places* in Christ."

And you are looked down upon and gossiped about by the other churchgoers in area that you may be struggling. Or they may experience when going to the pastor or leader of the church for help, only to have the information all over the church. That was my experience. Jesus delivered and healed all who came to him. I never saw him ask for anyone to sow a seed for deliverance or healing. Jesus allowed people of their own free will to support his ministry because they saw the results that Jesus was getting. We must follow God's laws, principles, statutes, and ordinances and to submit yourself to God so Satan will flee.

This book of the law shall not depart out of thy mouth; but thou shalt meditate therein day and night, that thou mayest observe to do according to all that is written therein: for then thou shalt make thy way prosperous, and then thou shalt have good success. (Joshua 1:8)

Blessed *is* the man that walketh not in the counsel of the ungodly, nor standeth in the way of sinners, nor sitteth in the seat of the scornful. But his delight *is* in the law of the Lord; and in his law doth he meditate day and night. And he shall be like a tree planted by the rivers of water, that bringeth forth his fruit in his season; his leaf also shall not wither; and whatsoever he doeth shall prosper. (Psalm 1:1–3)

We are constantly being bombarded with the things of the world; it is vital that we do what Romans 12:2 instructs us to do.

I beseech you therefore, brethren, by the mercies of God, that ye present your bodies a living sacrifice, holy, acceptable unto God, *which is* your reasonable service. And be not conformed to this world: but be ye transformed by the renewing of your mind, that ye may prove what *is* that good, and acceptable, and perfect, will of God. (Romans 12:1–2)

People are not our problem because of what Adam and Eve did in the Garden of Eden by eating from the forbidden tree. It made Satan the god of this world. "For we wrestle not against flesh and blood, but against principalities, against powers, against the rulers of the darkness of this world, against spiritual wickedness in high *places*" (Ephesians 6:12). So keep your armor on (Ephesians 6:10–18) by living a holy and godly life before our Heavenly Father. What I am saying is that people are not our problem.

We have to follow God's laws, principles, statutes, and ordinances and to submit ourself to God so that Satan can flee. "Submit yourselves therefore to God. Resist the devil, and he will flee from you" (James 4:7). When you fast, there are some things we are instructed to do in Isaiah 58:1–14:

> Cry aloud, spare not, lift up thy voice like a trumpet, and shew my people their transgression, and the house of Jacob their sins. Yet they seek me daily, and delight to know my ways, as a nation that did righteousness, and forsook not the ordinance of their God: they ask of me the ordinances of justice; they take delight in approaching to God. Wherefore have we fasted, *say they*, and thou seest not? *wherefore* have we afflicted our soul, and thou takest no knowledge? Behold, in the day of your fast ye find pleasure, and exact all your labours. Behold, ye fast for strife and debate, and to smite with the fist of wickedness: ye shall not fast as *ye do this* day, to make your voice to be heard on high. Is it such a fast that I have chosen? a day for a man to afflict his soul? *is it* to bow down his head as a bulrush, and to spread sackcloth and ashes *under him*? wilt thou call this a fast, and an acceptable day to the LORD? Is not this the fast that I have chosen? to loosen the bonds of wickedness, to undo the heavy burdens, and to let the oppressed go free, and that ye break every yoke? Is it not to deal thy bread to the hungry, and that thou bring the poor that are cast out to thy house? when thou seest the naked, that thou cover him; and that thou hide not thyself from thine own flesh? Then shall thy light break forth as the morning, and thine health shall spring forth speedily: and thy righteousness shall go before thee; the glory of the

Lord shall be thy reward. Then shalt thou call, and the Lord shall answer; thou shalt cry, and he shall say, Here I *am.* If thou take away from the midst of thee the yoke, the putting forth of the finger, and speaking vanity; And *if* thou draw out thy soul to the hungry, and satisfy the afflicted soul; then shall thy light rise in obscurity, and thy darkness *be* as the noon day: And the Lord shall guide thee continually, and satisfy thy soul in drought, and make fat thy bones: and thou shalt be like a watered garden, and like a spring of water, whose waters fail not. And they *that they shall be* of thee shall build the old waste places: *thou shalt raise up the foundations of many generations; and thou shalt be called, The repairer of the breach*, The restorer of paths to dwell in. If thou turn away thy foot from the sabbath, *from* doing thy pleasure on my holy day; and call the sabbath a delight, the holy of the Lord, honourable; and shalt honour him, not doing thine own ways, nor finding thine own pleasure, nor speaking *thine own* words: Then shalt thou delight thyself in the Lord; and I will cause thee to ride upon the high places of the earth, and feed thee with the heritage of Jacob thy father: for the mouth of the Lord hath spoken *it.*

When we follow the instructions of Isaiah 58, we are called the repairer of the breach. According to Leviticus 26:40, "If they shall confess their iniquity, and the iniquity of their fathers, with their trespass which they trespassed against me, and that also they have walked contrary unto me"; we have the authority to confess the iniquity of our fathers. Life is so much better and more free after deliverance. Thank you, God.

About the Author

Sheila White grew up in a family with eight other siblings with her mother and stepfather. She was raised to respect the difference in others that was out of their control. For example, if someone was disabled, she was taught not to treat them differently from anyone else. She grew up in a household with strict rules. That did not stop her from having her first and only child at sixteen. She wrote her first book when she was pregnant. That assignment was given to her by her teacher in a school for pregnant girls. She received an A on her first book, which came up missing after she allowed a family member to view the book. This current book and title were given to her to write by God. She was also given the title to several of the chapters the same day. She wrote this book to encourage others of what God can do in their life if they let him into their lives. There is also a chapter written to encourage women that they are just as important to God as the men are in the Bible.